ICONS

ARCHITECTURE NOW!

ARCHITECTURE NOW!

EDITOR **PHILIP JODIDIO**

KÖLN LONDON LOS ANGELES MADRID PARIS TOKYO

CONTENTS

PREFACE 006/007/008 ARCHITECTS TADAO ANDO 010/011 PAUL ANDREU 012/013 ANGÉLIL/GRAHAM/PFENNINGER/SCHOLL 014/015 ARCHITECTURE STUDIO 016/017 WIEL ARETS 018/019 ASYMPTOTE 020/021 SHIGERU BAN 022/023 BERGER + PARKKINEN 024/025 BOLLES + WILSON 026/027 BOORA ARCHITECTS 028/029 MARIO BOTTA 030/031 BRANSON COATES 032/033 WILL BRUDER 034/035 SANTIAGO CALATRAVA 036/037 ALBERTO CAMPO BAEZA 038/039 DAVID CHIPPERFIELD 040/041 CLARE DESIGN 042/043 COOP HIMMELB(L)AU 044/045 DALY GENIK 046/047 DILLER + SCOFIDIO 048/049 ERICK VAN EGERAAT 050/051 STEVEN EHRLICH 052/053 FREDERICK FISHER 054/055 NORMAN FOSTER 056/057 MASSIMILIANO FUKSAS 058/059 FRANK O. GEHRY 060/061 GIGON/GUYER 062/063 NICHOLAS GRIMSHAW 064/065 GROSE BRADLEY 066/067 ZAHA HADID 068/069 HIROSHI HARA 070/071 ITSUKO HASEGAWA 072/073 ZVI HECKER 074/075 HERZOG & DE MEURON 076/077 STEVEN HOLL 078/079 DAVID HOVEY 080/081 ARATA ISOZAKI 082/083 TOYO ITO 084/085 JAKOB + MACFARLANE 086/087 VINCENT JAMES 088/089 REI KAWAKUBO 090/091 KHRAS 092/093 WARO KISHI 094/095 JOSEF PAUL KLEIHUES 096/097 KOHN PEDERSEN FOX 098/099 REM KOOLHAAS 100/101

KENGO KUMA 102/103 LAMOTT ARCHITEKTEN 104/105 MAYA LIN 106/107
DANIEL LIBESKIND 108/109 FUMIHIKO MAKI 110/111 MECANOO 112/113
RICHARD MEIER 114/115 RAFAEL MONEO 116/117 TOSHIKO MORI 118/119
MORPHOSIS 120/121 ERIC OWEN MOSS 122/123 GLENN MURCUTT 124/125
MVRDV 126/127 TAKEHIKO NAGAKURA 128/129 NEUTELINGS RIEDIJK 130/131
JEAN NOUVEL 132/133 NOX 134/135 IEOH MING PEI 136/137 DOMINIQUE
PERRAULT 138/139 RENZO PIANO 140/141 POLSHEK PARTNERSHIP 142/143
CHRISTIAN DE PORTZAMPARC 144/145 ELISABETH DE PORTZAMPARC 146/147
RICHARD ROGERS 148/149 ROTO 150/151 MIKE RUNDELL AND DAMIEN HIRST
152/153 SCHMIDT, HAMMER & LASSEN 154/155 AXEL SCHULTES AND CHARLOTTE
FRANK 156/157 SCHWEGER+PARTNER 158/159 ALVARO SIZA 160/161 SKIDMORE,
OWINGS & MERRILL 162/163 EDUARDO SOUTO MOURA 164/165 THOMAS
SPIEGELHALTER 166/167 PHILIPPE STARCK 168/169 SHIN TAKAMATSU 170/171
YOSHIO TANIGUCHI 172/173 TEN ARQUITECTOS 174/175 BERNARD TSCHUMI
176/177 UN STUDIO 178/179 MAKOTO SEI WATANBE 180/181 WILLIAMS AND
TSIEN 182/183 JEAN-MICHEL WILMOTTE 184/185 KEN YEANG 186/187 SHOEI
YOH 188/189 *CREDITS* 190

PREFACE

Is it art, or is it architecture? Or then again, might it be fashion? Contemporary architecture has many of the qualities of other disciplines, but it is above all varied. In this book the work of eighty-seven different architects is presented, each of them with their own style, materials and regional influences. The buildings shown here are made of concrete (Tadao Ando), or of paper (Shigeru Ban); they are minimalist (Wiel Arets), sculptural (Frank Gehry), or even figurative (Branson Coates). Because they are selected precisely for the variety of their work, because each of these architects is important in his or her own way, the eighty-seven selected here can be considered to be today's most creative building designers. They are Australian, Japanese, American or European, but they are each engaged in solving the practical problems of a given client, site and function, while still adding something of their own personality, their own take on what makes architecture truly contemporary. And out of their diversity can be drawn an almost self-evident conclusion: today there is no International Style, no one way to view the present. Architecture is sometimes fashionable, surely more so in periods of economic prosperity than in the down cycles. Even questions as fundamental as the durability of a building meet with varying responses according to the region, the nature of the building, and the architect. The heavy concrete walls of Tadao Ando are made to resist the earthquakes of his native Japan, while Toshiko Mori seeks ways to help the homeless with temporary abodes made of cloth. Then too, ideas in architecture often take time to move from the drawing board to the completed structure. Pioneers of the so-called Deconstructivist style in the 1980s like Austria's Coop Himmelblau are today completing work whose inspiration will not seem outdated two or three trends later.

The American sculptor Richard Serra was once asked about the difference between art and architecture. He answered that "art serves no purpose." Obviously, architecture serves a purpose, and therein may lay its real interest. Artists, without the practical constraints imposed on even the most ephemeral building, are not obliged to take into account the needs of day to day life. Architecture is deeply anchored in reality, and obliged to face a public that is not the rarified gallery-going crowd that judges art. Architecture is for everyone; it is a place to live, to play, to eat, to take in culture, to move – it is the theatre of life. When John Ruskin wrote in the 19th century that architecture is the greatest of the arts, he meant that good architecture had to make use of other art forms, creating a whole that, ideally, would be the high point of human creativity. Architects no longer find it necessary to associate themselves with other artists to achieve what in and of itself can be considered an artistic expression. Architecture can be art, as Frank Gehry's best work perhaps shows, which does not mean that it is no longer "condemned" to serve a purpose.

Technology is transforming the way buildings are designed and built as surely as it has changed other areas. Gehry has in fact been a precursor in the use of software to design and build, as he did with Dassault's Catia program for the Guggenheim Bilbao. But Frank Gehry is of the generation that came late to accept the computer as a useful tool for the execution of a design that has more to do with a sketchpad than it does with a screen. Other younger architects, from New York's Asymptote group to Holland's NOX and MvRdV, are coming closer to the goal of work that is truly inspired by the new possibilities

PREFACE

offered by CAD. In their hands, the computer is not simply a tool to make building easier, it is an integral part of the design process, an open door to new worlds where non-Euclidean forms are as natural as cubes and spheres were to a younger generation. This is a real revolution that some would like to carry as far as a virtual architecture that would never be intended as anything other than an interactive image on a screen. This is the idea behind the "Virtual Guggenheim" proposed by Asymptote, a museum that would change in function of its visitors needs, a "building" that would never need to actually be built.

The younger Dutch architects and some Japanese figures such as Makoto Sei Watanabe have also practiced interactivity in various forms. The Water Pavilion on the artificial island of Neeltje Jans in the Dutch province of Zeeland, by NOX and Oosterhuis Associates, was one of the first ventures into interactive, computer-designed architecture to actually be built. There is likely to be much more of this, even if there is a certain amount of frenzy around newly found "gadgets," which may well be left by the wayside as computers truly come into their own as an integral part of the architectural design of the future. Much of the built work shown in this volume nonetheless testifies to the formidable acceleration of change in architecture. Driven by computers or by the desire to improve on ideas that have their origin in the modern period, this is…. Architecture Now.

PHILIP JODIDIO
29 March 2002

ARCHITECTS

TADAO ANDO

"When I was 15, I saw a book on the complete work of Le Corbusier. I recopied some of his drawings, and that is how I began to be interested in architecture."

Born in Osaka in 1941, Tadao Ando was self-educated as an architect, largely through his travels in the United States, Europe and Africa (1962–69). He founded Tadao Ando Architect & Associates in Osaka in 1969. He has received the Alvar Aalto Medal, Finnish Association of Architects (1985); Medaille d'or, French Academy of Architecture (1989); the 1992 Carlsberg Prize and the 1995 Pritzker Prize. He has taught at Yale (1987); Columbia (1988) and at Harvard (1990). Notable buildings include: Rokko Housing, Kobe (1983–93); Church on the Water, Hokkaido (1988); Japan Pavilion Expo '92, Seville, Spain (1992); Forest of Tombs Museum, Kumamoto (1992); and the Suntory Museum, Osaka (1994). Recent work includes the Awaji Yumebutai, Awajishima, Hyogo, Japan (1997–2000); the Modern Art Museum of Fort Worth, Fort Worth, Texas, United States (1999–2002); and the Pulitzer Foundation for the Arts, Saint-Louis, Missouri, 1997–2000. He recently won the competition to design the new Pinault Foundation on the Ile Seguin, Paris, France.

01 CHICAGO HOUSE, Chicago, Illinois, USA, 1992–97. **02 AWAJI YUMEBUTAI,** Awajishima, Hyogo, Japan, 1995–2000/03.
03 TOTO SEMINAR HOUSE, Tsuna-Gun, Hyogo, Japan, 1994–97.

01

PAUL ANDREU

An architect and an engineer, Paul Andreu speaks of the "poetry of construction," and he views each new project as a series of structural problems that must be resolved.

Paul Andreu was born on July 10, 1938 in Caudéran in the Gironde region of France. He obtained diplomas from the École Polytechnique (1961), the École Nationale des Ponts et Chaussées (1963, as an engineer) and as an architect from the École des Beaux Arts in Paris (1968). As Chief Architect of the Aéroports de Paris he has been responsible not only for the development of Charles de Gaulle (Roissy) Airport, but also for the development of approximately 50 airports around the world such as those of Jakarta (1986); Teheran (1996); Harare, Zimbabwe (1996) or more recently still, Shanghai-Pudong. Andreu has also worked on other large scale projects such as the French terminal for the Eurotunnel project (1987) and currently the Beijing Opera House. Other current work includes the Museum of Maritime History of Osaka, Japan.

01 NATIONAL GRAND THEATER OF CHINA, Beijing, China, 1999–2002. **02/03 ROISSY 2F**, Paris, France, 1990–98.

02/03

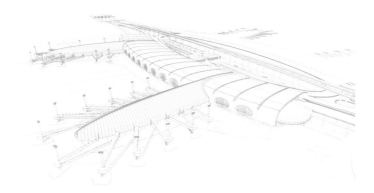

ANGÉLIL/GRAHAM/ PFENNINGER/SCHOLL

Though minimalist, this group's work is full of spatial surprises.

Marc Angélil studied at the ETH in Zurich (1973–79) before obtaining a doctorate from the same institution in 1987. He has been a professor at Harvard (1982–87); USC (1987–94) and at the ETH since 1999. Sarah Graham received her Bachelor of Arts degree from Stanford (1970–74), and her Masters from Harvard (1979–82). She was a Professor at the University of Southern California from 1987 to 1996. Angélil/Graham was founded in 1982 in Los Angeles. AGPS was established in 1990 in Zurich. Reto Pfenninger studied in Winterthur (1984–87) before working in Lausanne and at the Akademie der Bildenden Künste in Munich (1989–92). Manuel Scholl studied at the ETH in Zurich (1982–88) before working in architectural offices in Zurich and Barcelona. The firm's projects include the Midfield Airport Terminal, Zurich-Kloten (2000–2003); the renovation and new construction of apartments, offices and shops at Waschanstalt Zurich-Wollishofen (1999–2000); and the Herzo Base with Adidas "World of Sports," masterplan 2000.

01-03 TRÜB HOUSE, HT 96.4, Horgen, Switzerland, 1996–98.

01

ARCHITECTURE STUDIO

The work of Architecture Studio shows that contemporary architecture and a certain spirituality are by no means incompatible.

Created in 1973, Architecture Studio has six principals: Rodo Tisnado, Martin Robain, Alain Bretagnolle, René-Henri Arnaud, Jean-François Bonne and Laurent-Marc Fischer. Their first major building was the Institut du Monde Arabe (1981–87) designed with Nouvel, Soria and Lezènes. Other significant buildings include the Embassy of France in Muscat, Oman (1987–89); the Lycée du Futur, Jaunay-Clan, France (1986–87); the University Restaurant, Dunkirk, France (1991–93). Aside from Our Lady of the Ark of the Covenant, Paris, 1996–98; recent work includes the Institut national du Judo; Paris, France (1988–2000); the extension of the Exhibition Park at Paris-Nord Villepinte, 2000; and above all, the 220,000 square meter European Parliament in Strasbourg, France (1994–98).

01/02 OUR LADY OF THE ARK OF THE COVENANT, Paris, France, 1996–97.

WIEL ARETS

"I believe we are sooner a child of our times than born in a certain place. We travel around, teach, and are influenced by things that happen all over the world."

Born in Heerlen, in the Netherlands in 1955, Wiel Arets graduated from the Technical University in Eindhoven in 1983. He established Wiel Arets Architect & Associates in Heerlen in 1984. He traveled to Russia, Japan, America, and Europe (1984–89) and taught at the Academy of Architecture, Amsterdam, and Rotterdam (1986). His interest in architectural theory led him to create the publishing house Wiederhall in 1987. Arets was a Diploma Unit Master at the Architectural Association in London (1988–92); and a Visiting Professor at Columbia University (New York, 1991–92). He was Dean of the Berlage Institute, Postgraduate Laboratory of Architecture in Amsterdam (1995–98), where he was the successor of Herman Hertzberger. His built work includes a House & Pharmacy (Schoonbroodt, Brunssum, 1985–86); Barbershop and House (Mayntz, Heerlen, 1986–87); Fashionshop Beltgens (Maastricht, 1987); Academy of Art and Architecture (Maastricht, 1989–93); 67 apartments (Tilburg, 1992–94); the Headquarters of the AZL Pensionfund (Heerlen, 1990–95); a Police Station in Vaals, (1993–96); 104 apartments at Jacobsplaats (Rotterdam, 1995–97); and the Lensvelt Factory and Offices (Breda, 1999–2000).

01/02 LENSVELT FACTORY AND OFFICES, Breda, Netherlands, 1995–2000.

01/02 ►

ASYMPTOTE

While some architects feel that computers are useful only for some tasks, others have begun to explore radical new ideas such as the "virtual" building – one that will exist only on screens.

Lise Ann Couture was born in Montreal in 1959. She received her Bachelor of Architecture degree from Carlton University, Canada, and her Master of Architecture degree from Yale. She has been a Design Critic in the Master of Architecture program at Parsons School of Design, New York. Hani Rashid received his degree as Master of Architecture from the Cranbrook Academy of Art, Bloomfield Hills, Michigan. They created Asymptote in 1987. Projects include their 1988 prize winning commission for the Los Angeles West Coast Gateway 1989; a commissioned housing project for Brig, Switzerland; and their participation in the 1993 competition for an Art Center in Tours, France (1993). Other work by Asymptote includes a theater festival structure built in Denmark in 1997. Presently Asymptote is designing a Technology Museum in Kyoto, Japan, and the Guggenheim Virtual Museum.

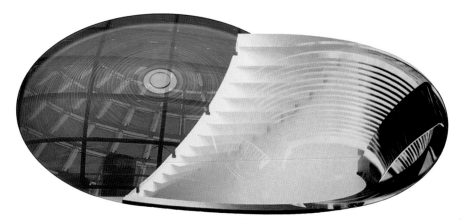

01

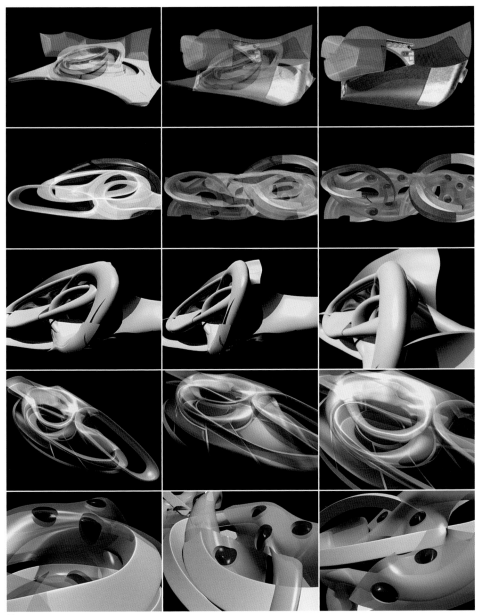

01/02 GUGGENHEIM, Virtual Museum, New York, NY, USA, 1999–2002.

SHIGERU BAN

Shigeru Ban has been a pioneer in the area of paper architecture – buildings whose primary structural material is paper.

Born in 1957 in Tokyo, Shigeru Ban studied at the Southern California Institute of Architecture (SciArc) from 1977 to 1980. He attended the Cooper Union School of Architecture, where he studied under John Hejduk (1980–82). He worked in the office of Arata Isozaki (1982–83) before founding his own firm in Tokyo in 1985. His work includes numerous exhibition designs (Alvar Aalto show at the Axis Gallery, Tokyo, 1986). His buildings include the Odawara Pavilion, Kanagawa, 1990; the Paper Gallery, Tokyo, 1994; the Paper House, Lake Yamanaka, 1995; and the Paper Church, Takatori, Hyogo, 1995. He has also designed ephemeral structures such as his Paper Refugee Shelter made with plastic sheets and paper tubes for the United Nations High Commissioner for Refugees (UNHCR). He designed the Japanese Pavilion at Expo 2000 in Hannover. Current work includes a small museum of Canal History in Pouilly-en-Auxois, France, and housing in Beijing, China.

01-03 PAPER HOUSE, Lake Yamanaka, Yamanashi, Japan, 1994–95.

01

BERGER + PARKKINEN

The Austrian-Finnish partnership of Alfred Berger and Tiina Parkkinen won the 1995 competition to design the master plan for the embassies of the five Nordic countries in Berlin.

Alfred Berger is Austrian and Tiina Parkkinen is Finnish, although she was born in Vienna in 1965, where she attended the Akademie der Bildenden Künste, graduating in 1994. Alfred Berger was born in Salzburg in 1961, and attended the Technical University in Vienna before going on to the Akademie der Bildenden Künste, which he left in 1989. He established his first architectural office, Berger & Krismer, in 1990, followed by Penttilä-Berger-Krismer in 1992. They founded Berger + Parkkinen in 1995. Their work includes the Ice Stadium (Vienna, 1994), the renovation of the Akademie der Bildenden Künste (1998), and the master plan of the Nordic Embassies in Berlin Germany. Current projects include a Biomedical research center in Vienna and a Court House in Leoben, Austria (2000).

01/02 NORDIC EMBASSIES, Berlin, Germany, 1995–99.

BOLLES + WILSON

Located near the Erasmus Bridge by Ben van Berkel, the quay buildings designed by
Bolles + Wilson signal the amplitude of the development of the Kop van Zuid area,
the former docks of Rotterdam.

Peter Wilson was born in Melbourne in 1950. He studied at the University of Melbourne
(1968–70), and at the Architectural Association in London (1972–74). Julia Bolles Wilson was born
in 1948 in Münster, and studied at the University of Karlsruhe (1968–76) and at the A.A. in London
(1978–79) while Wilson was Unit Master (1978–88). They formed the Wilson Partnership in London in
1980, and Architekturbüro Bolles+Wilson in 1987. The office moved in 1988 to Münster. Their projects
include a "Garden folly" at Expo '90 in Osaka. Peter Wilson built the Suzuki House (1993), Tokyo. Other
recent projects include the WLV Office Building in Münster, Germany (1991–96); the Kop van Zuid Quay
Buildings in Rotterdam (1991–96), the Volksbank Borken Headquarters, Borken, Germany (1997–2000);
and the TGZ II Laboratory in Halle-Wittenberg, Germany (1999–2000).

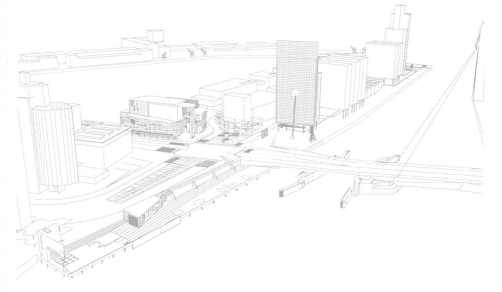

02

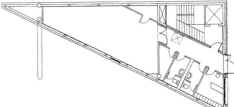

01-03 QUAY BUILDINGS, Kop van Zuid,
Rotterdam, The Netherlands, 1991–96.

03

BOORA ARCHITECTS

This prototype of a "quick service restaurant featuring healthy haute cuisine and specialty drinks to go," designed for a site on the Pacific Coast Highway, breaks new ground.

Created in 1960, Boora Architects is managed by nine principals and has a staff of 100 persons. The firm does architectural, planning and interior design work both in the United States and in other countries. They have completed master plans and buildings for thirty-four college and university campuses and sixty-five performing arts spaces. Current work includes the new performing arts center for the University of California, Davis; the National Underground Railroad Freedom Center, Cincinnati, Ohio; the Arts and Entertainment Center, Mesa, Arizona; and the Mark O. Hatfield Courthouse, Portland, Oregon.

01-04 **AUTOBISTRO**, Newport Beach, California, USA, 1997–98.

01

02

03/04 ►

MARIO BOTTA

"I love churches because they make you feel that you are the protagonist. In fact, you must be able to enter a church and feel that you are at the center of the world."

Born in Mendrisio, Switzerland (1943), Mario Botta left school at 15 to become apprentice in a Lugano architectural office – and designed his first house the following year. After studies in Milan and Venice, he worked briefly in the entourage of Le Corbusier, Louis Kahn and Luigi Snozzi. He has built private houses in Cadenazzo (1970–71), Riva San Vitale (1971–73), or Ligornetto (1975–76). Major buildings include: Médiathèque (Villeurbanne, 1984–88); Cultural Center (Chambéry, 1982–87); Évry Cathedral (1988–1995); San Francisco Museum of Modern Art (1992–95); Tamaro Chapel (Monte Tamaro, Switzerland, 1992–96); Tinguely Museum (Basel, 1993–96); Chapel (Mogno, Switzerland, 1986–98), and a design for the renovation of the Presbytery of the Cathedral of Santa Maria del Fiore (Florence, 1997).

01-03 CHURCH OF SAINT JOHN THE BAPTIST, Mogno, Ticino, Switzerland, 1986 / 92–98.

BRANSON COATES

Although Branson Coates has made surprising structures in the past, this figurative pavilion is undoubtedly one of the most unexpected elements to be found inside London's Millennium Dome.

Doug Branson, born in 1951, and Nigel Coates, born in 1949, formed Branson Coates in 1983 and both taught at the Architectural Association in London. Coates taught at the AA for many years, first as an assistant to Bernard Tschumi and then as Unit Master of Unit 10 (1977–89). The work of Branson Coates includes the Bohemia Jazz Club, Tokyo, 1986; Caffé Bongo, Tokyo, 1986; the Nishi Azubu Wall, Tokyo, 1990; and the Nautilus Bar and Seafood Restaurant at Schipol Airport, Netherlands, 1993. One of their most recent buildings is the National Center for Popular Music in Sheffield (1996–98), whose quatre-foil form inspired that of Powerhouse::UK, an inflatable, temporary structure built for the Department of Trade and Industry on Horse Guards Parade in 1998. Current work includes the refurbishment of the King Street offices of the auctioneers Christie's in London.

01/02 THE BODY ZONE, Millennium Dome, London, England, 2000.

WILL BRUDER

"The design concept of this residence is one of creating a series of abstract canyon walls of concrete masonry, emerging like geological gestures from the home's natural desert site."

Born in Milwaukee, Wisconsin in 1946, Will Bruder has a B.A. degree in Sculpture from the University of Wisconsin-Milwaukee and is self trained as an architect. He apprenticed under Paolo Soleri and Gunnar Birkerts. He obtained his architecture licence in 1974 and created his own studio the same year. He studied at the American Academy in Rome for six months in 1987. He has taught and lectured at SciArc, Yale, Taliesin West and Georgia Tech. His most important built work is the Phoenix Central Library in Phoenix, Arizona, 1988–95. Recent projects include Teton County Library, Jackson, Wyoming; Riddell Advertising, Jackson, Wyoming; Temple Kol Ami, Scottsdale, Arizona; Deer Vallery Rock Art Center, Phoenix, Arizona; and residences in Boston, Colorado, Arizona, Canada and Australia, as well as a restaurant in Manhattan.

01-05 BYRNE RESIDENCE, North Scottsdale, Arizona, USA, 1994–98.

01

02

03/04/05

SANTIAGO CALATRAVA

"They used to say that form follows function, but form has to do with other things too. Thank God, the toilets in my buildings work, so do the entrances and the exits. But where were the toilets in the Parthenon?"

Born in Valencia in 1951, Santiago Calatrava studied art and architecture at the Escuela Técnica Superior de Arquitectura in Valencia (1968–73) and engineering at the ETH in Zurich (doctorate in Technical Science, 1981). He opened his own architecture and civil engineering office the same year. His built work includes Gallery and Heritage Square, BCE Place, Toronto, 1987; the Bach de Roda Bridge, Barcelona, 1985–87; the Torre de Montjuic, Barcelona, 1989–92; the Kuwait Pavilion at Expo '92, Seville, and

01 ORIENTE STATION, Lisbon, Portugal, 1993–98.
02 CITY OF ARTS AND SCIENCES, Valencia, Spain, 1991–.

the Alamillo Bridge for the same exhibition; and the Lyon Satolas TGV Station, 1989–94. He completed the Oriente Station in Lisbon in 1998. He was a finalist in the competition for the Reichstag in Berlin, and he recently completed the Valencia City of Science and Planetarium, (Valencia, Spain, 1996–2000); the Sondica Airport (Bilbao, Spain, 1990–2000); and a bridge in Orléans (1996–2000). He is currently working on the Oakland Diocese Cathedral in California.

02

ALBERTO CAMPO BAEZA

This center gives a very distinct impression of a minimal style that the architect goes so far as to call its "CB flavor" (after his own initials).

Born in Cadiz, Alberto Campo Baeza studied in Madrid where he obtained his Ph.D. in 1982. He has taught in Madrid, at the ETH in Zurich (1989–90), at Cornell University, and at the University of Pennsylvania (1986 and 1999). His work includes the Fene Town Hall (1980); S. Fermin Public School, Madrid (1985); Public Library, Orihuela (1992); a Public School, Cadiz (1992); the BIT Center in Mallorca (1998); and a number of private houses. Current work includes the headquarters for "La Caja General de Ahorros" in Granada, and a house for Tom Ford of Gucci in Santa Fe, New Mexico.

01-03 CENTER FOR INNOVATIVE TECHNOLOGIES BIT,
Inca, Majorca, Spain, 1995–98.

DAVID CHIPPERFIELD

This clothing shop was inserted into the ground and first floors of a 1960s office block at 74 Sloane Avenue, just around the corner from the landmark Michelin "Bibendum" building.

Born in London in 1953, David Chipperfield obtained his Diploma in Architecture from the Architectural Association (AA, London, 1977). He worked in offices of Norman Foster and Richard Rogers, before establishing David Chipperfield Architects (London, 1984). Built work includes: Arnolfini Arts Center (Bristol, 1987); Design Store (Kyoto, 1989); Matsumoto Headquarters Building (Okayama, Japan, 1990); Plant Gallery and Central Hall of the Natural History Museum (London, 1993); Wagamama Restaurant (London, 1996); River & Rowing Museum (Henley-on-Thames, 1996). His current work includes: Landeszentralbank (Gera, Germany); Housing (Berlin Spandau); Office Building (Dusseldorf); and reconstruction of the Neues Museum (Berlin, 2000–06).

01   02

01-04 JOSEPH MEN'S SHOP, London, England, 1997.

CLARE DESIGN

"We wanted the guts and ruggedness of the farm shed and the lightness and openness of a surf club."

Lindsay Clare was born in 1952 in Brisbane, and Kerry Clare was born in Sydney in 1957. They both obtained their degrees in architecture from the Queensland University of Technology, and set up their practice in Mooloolabe in 1980. Their built work includes more than one hundred projects such as the McWilliam Residence, Sunshine Coast, 1990; Clare Residence, Sunshine Coast, 1991; Hammond Residence, Sunshine Coast, 1994; and Cotton Tree Pilot Housing, Sunshine Coast, 1995. They have

01/02 SUNSHINE COAST UNIVERSITY CLUB, Sippy Downs, Queensland, Australia, 1996.

attempted to "combine principles of modernism and traditional Queensland architecture in order to generate solutions that respond to environment, contemporary culture and community needs." Lindsay and Kerry Clare are currently working as Design Directors for the New South Wales Government Architect. Current projects include the Sydney Cove Waterfront Strategy, the Royal Botanic Gardens Exhibition Centre, the Olympic Village School and the Environment Centre for the Riverina Institute of TAFE.

COOP HIMMELB(L)AU

The building is "designed like a video-clip and seeks to do away with centralized perspective."

Wolf Prix and Helmut Swiczinsky founded Coop Himmelblau in 1968 in Vienna, Austria. In 1988, they opened a second office in Los Angeles. Wolf Prix was born in 1942 in Vienna, and educated at the Technische Universität, Vienna, the Southern California Institute of Architecture (SCI-Arc), and the Architectural Association (AA), London. He has been a Professor of the Masterclass of Architecture at the University of Applied Arts, Vienna, and an Adjunct Professor at SCI-Arc. Helmut Swiczinsky, born in 1944 in Poznan, Poland, was raised in Vienna and educated at the Technische Universität, Vienna, and at the AA, London. Completed projects of the group include the Rooftop Remodeling in Vienna; masterplan for Mélun-Sénart, France; and the East Pavilion of the Groninger Museum, Groningen, The Netherlands, 1990–94. They also remodeled the Austrian Pavilion in the Giardini, Venice, Italy. Recent work includes the Museum of Health, Dresden, the Academy of Fine Arts, Munich, the UFA Cinema Center (Dresden, Germany, 1997–98), and the SEG Apartment Tower, Vienna.

01/02 UFA CINEMA CENTER, Dresden, Germany, 1996–98.

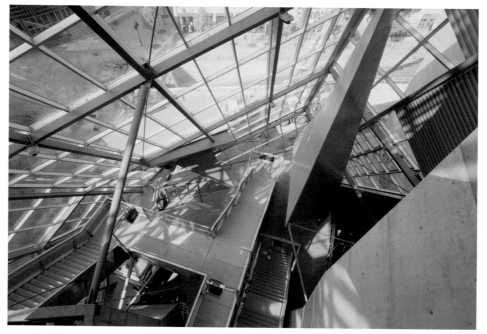

The combination of aluminum and concrete gives the house an almost industrial look that seems inspired by temporary housing or shipping containers.

Chris Genik received his Bachelor of Architecture degree from Carleton University (1983) and his Master of Architecture from Rice University (1985). Following graduate school, he formed a partnership with Rice University professor Peter Waldman and undertook a series of institutional, residential, and theoretical projects. While practicing he held a teaching position at the University of Houston. He moved to Los Angeles to create Daly Genik in 1989. Kevin Daly received his Master of Architecture degree at Rice University and his Bachelor of Architecture at the University of California Berkeley. He has participated in the studio faculty of the Southern California Institute of Architecture (1992–1999). Before becoming a principal of Daly Genik in 1989, he worked as an associate in the office of Frank O. Gehry (1986–90); with Hodgetts & Fung (1985–86); and at the Design Build Studio in Berkeley (1980–85).

01

02

03

04

01-04 VALLEY CENTER HOUSE, North San Diego County,
California, USA, 1998.

DILLER + SCOFIDIO

"Since man can no longer claim to be in the center of a controllable universe, the position of the spectator continues to be an issue of critical reflection."

Elizabeth Diller is Professor of Architecture at Princeton University and Ricardo Scofidio is Professor of Architecture at The Cooper Union in New York. According to their own description, "Diller + Scofidio is a collaborative, interdisciplinary studio involved in architecture, the visual arts and the performing arts. The team is primarily involved in thematically-driven experimental works that take the form of architectural commissions, temporary installations and permanent site-specific installations, multi-media theater, electronic media, and print." Their work includes "Slither," 100 units of social housing in Gifu, Japan, and "Moving Target," a collaborative dance work with Charleroi/Danse Belgium. Installations by Diller + Scofidio have been seen at the Cartier Foundation in Paris (Master/Slave, 1999); the Museum of Modern Art in New York or the Musée de la Mode in Paris. Recently, they completed The Brasserie Restaurant (Seagram Building, New York, 1998–1999); the Blur Building, (Expo 02, Yverdon-les-Bains, Switzerland, 2000–02) and were selected as architects for the Institute of Contemporary Art in Boston.

01 THE BRASSERIE, Seagram Building, New York, NY, USA, 1998–2000.
02 BLUR BUILDING, International Expo 2002, Yverdon, Switzerland, 1998–2002.

01

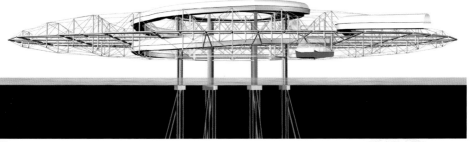

ERICK VAN EGERAAT

"A modest manifesto against the repressive effect of misplaced and carping conservatism and in favor of reinterpretation using contemporary means."

Erick van Egeraat was born in 1956 in Amsterdam. He created Mecanoo architects with Henk Döll, Chris de Weijer and Francine Houben in Delft in 1983. Their work included large housing projects such as the Herdenkingsplein in Maastricht (1990–92), and smaller scale projects such as their 1990 Boompjes Pavilion, a cantilevered structure overlooking the harbor of Rotterdam. He left Mecanoo in 1995 with 17 members of the staff and created Erick van Egeraat Associated Architects. He has declared his intention to go towards a "warm, inviting architecture," which he calls "Modern Baroque" as opposed to a more neo-modern style favored by Mecanoo. Their work includes the Pop art Exhibition, Kunsthal, Rotterdam, 1995; Housing Sternstrasse, Dresden (1994–); Leonardo da Vinci exhibition design, Rotterdam 1995–96; reconstruction of the 'Grote Markt' square east, Groningen; Utrecht Centrum Project, masterplan 1995–96, and the School for Fashion and Graphic Industry in Utrecht (1994–97). More recent projects are the renovation and extension of the Haarlem Theater (2001–05); an art gallery and public square for Middlesbrough (2002–05) and the Alphen aan den Rijn City Hall (1997–2002).

01-03 SCHOOL FOR FASHION AND GRAPHIC INDUSTRY, Utrecht, The Netherlands, 1994–97.

01

02/03 ▶

STEVEN EHRLICH

"I'd like to think the pavilion, with the new materials and the evaporating glass walls, takes Neutra's ideas a step further."

Born in New York in 1946, Steven Ehrlich received his B.Arch. degree from the Rensselaer Poly-technic Institute, Troy, New York in 1969. He studied indigenous vernacular architecture in North and West Africa from 1969 to 1977. He has completed numerous private residences, including the Friedman Residence (1986), the Ehrman-Coombs Residence (1989–1991, Santa Monica), and the Schulman Residence (Brentwood, 1989–1992) all in the Los Angeles area. Other built work includes the Shatto Recreation Center (Los Angeles, 1991); Sony Music Entertainment Campus (Santa Monica, 1993); Child Care Center for Sony, Culver City (1993–95); Game Show Network, Culver City (1995) as well as the Robertson Branch Library (Los Angeles, 1996). More recently, he has worked on the DreamWorks SKG Animation Studios, Glendale, California, 1998; the Orange Coast Collage Art Center, Costa Mesa, 2000; and the Biblioteca Latinoamericana & Washington Youth Center, San Jose, 1999.

01/02 CANYON RESIDENCE, Los Angeles, California, USA, 1996–98.
03 HOUSE EXTENSION, Santa Monica, California, United States, 1996–98.

01

FREDERICK FISHER

At P.S.1, with an $8.5 million budget, Fisher provided 11,000 square meters of space, including unusual exterior exhibition "rooms" formed by concrete walls in front of the entrance.

Born in Cleveland, Ohio, in 1949, Frederick Fisher attended Oberlin College graduating in 1971, and entered the UCLA Graduate School of Architecture and Urban Planning the same year. He worked in the office of Frank Gehry in Santa Monica from 1978 to 1980. He created the firm Fisher/Roberts with UCLA classmate Thane Roberts before setting up his own independent practice. His work includes the Eli Broad Family Foundation, a renovation of a 1927 structure in Santa Monica, 1989; the L.A. Louver Gallery in Venice, California, 1994; P.S.1 in Long Island City, New York, 1988–97; and a number of private residences in California; as well as the West Shinjuku Studio Apartments, Tokyo, 1990.

01-03 P.S. 1, Long Island City, New York, New York,
United States, 1995–98.

NORMAN FOSTER

"You don't have to show everything. I think that it is a value judgment between what you reveal and what you don't reveal. There is nothing less sexy than a woman with nothing on..."

Born in Manchester, 1935, Norman Foster studied Architecture and City Planning at Manchester University (1961). He was awarded Henry Fellowship to Yale University, where he received M. Arch. degree and met Richard Rogers with whom he created Team 4. Royal Gold Medal for Architecture (1983); knighted in 1990; American Institute of Architects Gold Medal for Architecture (1994). Sir Norman Foster has notably built: IBM Pilot Head Office, Cosham (1970–71); Sainsbury Center for Visual Arts and Crescent Wing, University of East Anglia, Norwich (1976–77; 1989–91); Hong Kong and Shanghai Banking Corporation Headquarters, Hong Kong (1981–86); London's Third Airport, Stansted (1987–91); University of Cambridge, Faculty of Law, Cambridge (1993–95); Commerzbank Headquarters, Frankfurt, Germany (1994–97). Recent projects include: Airport at Chek Lap Kok, Hong Kong (1995–98); New German Parliament, Reichstag, Berlin, Germany (1995–99); British Museum Redevelopment, London (1997–2000).

01 GREATER LONDON AUTHORITY, London, England, 1999–2002. **02/03 REICHSTAG**, Berlin, Germany, 1993–99.

01

MASSIMILIANO FUKSAS

"The influence of art on architecture should not be immediately visible. I don't like obvious sources of inspiration. Inspiration should be sentimental, intellectual or affective."

Born in Rome in 1944, Massimiliano Fuksas received his degree from the Faculty of Architecture in Rome in 1969. Created the architectural office "Granma" with Anna Maria Sacconi (1969–1988). Having completed a large number of projects in Italy, he began to be known in both Italy and France as of the late 1980s with projects such as his New Cemetery in Orvieto (1990), the Town Hall and Library of Cassino (1990) and in France, the Médiathèque, Rézé (1991), and the École nationale d'Ingénieurs de Brest (ENIB, 1992). More recently, he completed the restructuring of a city block on the Rue Candie in Paris (1987–93). Recent work includes the Lycée Technique in Alfortville, and the Place des Nations in Geneva, a 150 meter high tower in Vienna, and a large shopping center in Salzburg. Massimiliano Fuksas was appointed Director of the Venice Architecture Biennial for a four year period beginning in 1999.

01/02 EUROPARK SPAR, Salzburg, Austria, 1994–97.

FRANK O. GEHRY

> "I think artistic expression is the juice that fuels our collective souls, that innovation and responding to desperate social needs are not exclusive imperatives."

Born in Toronto, Canada in 1929, Frank Gehry, studied at the University of Southern California, Los Angeles (1949–51), and at Harvard (1956–57). Principal of Frank O. Gehry and Associates, Inc., Los Angeles, since 1962, he received the 1989 Pritzker Prize. Some of his notable projects are the Loyola Law School, Los Angeles (1981–84); the Norton Residence, Venice, California (1983); California Aerospace Museum, Los Angeles (1982–84); Schnabel Residence, Brentwood (1989); Festival Disney, Marne-la-Vallée, France (1989–92); Guggenheim Museum, Bilbao Spain (1991–97); Experience Music Project (Seattle, Washington, 1995–2000); and the as yet unbuilt Guggenheim Museum (New York, 1998–).

01/02 EXPERIENCE MUSIC PROJECT, Seattle, Washington, USA, 1995–2000.

GIGON/GUYER

> The sawtooth roof naturally serves to facilitate the natural lighting, but it also echoes local industrial architecture or even the mountainous countryside.

Born in 1959, Annette Gigon received her diploma from the ETH in Zurich in 1984. She worked in the office of Herzog & de Meuron in Basel (1985–88) before setting up her own practice (1987–89) and creating her present firm with Mike Guyer in 1989. Born in 1958, Mike Guyer also graduated from the ETH in 1984, and worked with Rem Koolhaas (OMA) (1984–87), and then taught with Hans Kollhoff at ETH (1987–88). Their built work includes the Kirchner Museum (Davos, 1990–92); the Vinikus Restaurant (Davos, 1990–92); and a renovation of the Oskar Reinhart Collection (Römerholz, Winterthur, 1997–98). Gigon/Guyer have participated in numerous international competitions such as for the Nelson-Atkins Museum extension (Kansas, 1999), or the Santiago de Compostela "City of Culture" project (1999). Current work includes the extension of the Aviation/Space Museum in Lucerne (2000–2003). The office currently employs a total of 18 architects.

01-03 MUSEUM LINER, Appenzell, Switzerland, 1996–98.

01

NICHOLAS GRIMSHAW

The Eden Project is a "showcase for global bio-diversity and human dependence upon plants." It is made up of "linked, climate-controlled transparent capsules set in a design landscape."

A 1965 graduate of the Architectural Association, Nicholas Grimshaw was born in 1939 in London. He created his present firm, Nicholas Grimshaw and Partners Ltd. in 1980. His numerous factory structures include those built for Herman Miller in Bath (1976), BMW at Bracknell (1980), the furniture maker Vitra at Weil-am-Rhein, Germany (1981), or for The Financial Times in London in 1988. He also built houses associated with the Sainsbury Supermarket Development in Camden Town (1989), and the British Pavilion at the 1992 Universal Exhibition in Seville. One of his most visible works is the International Terminal of Waterloo Station, 1988–93. Other work includes the Ludwig Erhard Haus (Berlin, Germany, 1996–98); or the Health and Medical Sciences (EIHMS) building at the University of Surrey; and the RAC Regional Headquarters in Bristol.

01-03 THE EDEN PROJECT, St. Austell, Cornwall, England, 1998–2000.

01

GROSE BRADLEY

Clad largely in glass in order to permit the owner to fully enjoy the view, the house sits on a platform, highlighting the architects' desire not to disturb the natural environment.

James Grose was born in 1954 in Brisbane. He is a Chartered Architect in Queensland and New South Wales. He was Director of Grose Bradley PL from 1988 to 1998, and is presently a Principal of Bligh Voller Nield. His work includes numerous private houses such as the McMullen House, Toowoon Bay, 1989; the A3 House, Sydney, 1991; the Myer House, Rocky Point, 1992; the Granger House, Oxford Falls, 1996; as well as the Steel House, Mooball, 1997, for which he received a 1998 Award for Outstanding Architecture. He worked on Facility Buildings for the Sydney 2000 Olympic Games. A monograph on the work of Grose Bradley was published in 1998 by L'Arcaedizioni, Milan, under the title *The Poetics of Materiality*.

01-03 STEEL HOUSE, Mooball, New South Wales, Australia, 1996–97.

ZAHA HADID

With its terraces and walkways, the building seems not to be an alien presence as its complex design might have implied, and as Zaha Hadid's reputation might have led some to expect.

Zaha Hadid studied architecture at the Architectural Association in London (AA) beginning in 1972 and was awarded the Diploma Prize in 1977. She then became a partner of Rem Koolhaas in the Office for Metropolitan Architecture (OMA) and taught at the AA. She has also taught at Harvard, the University of Chicago, in Hamburg and at Columbia University in New York. Well known for her paintings and drawings, she has had a substantial influence despite having built relatively few buildings. She has completed

01 LANDSCAPE FORMATION ONE, Weil am Rhein, Germany, 1996–99.
02 MIND ZONE, Millennium Dome, London, England, 1999.

the Vitra Fire Station, Weil-am-Rhein, Germany, 1990–94, and exhibition designs such as for "The Great Utopia," Solomon R. Guggenheim Museum, New York, 1992. Significant competition entries include her design for the Cardiff Bay Opera House, 1994–96; the Habitable Bridge, London, 1996; or the Luxembourg Philharmonic Hall, Luxembourg, 1997.

HIROSHI HARA

The Kyoto JR Station hints at the reality of the theories of Hara, who has written about future cities made of interconnected skyscrapers.

Born in Kawasaki, Japan, in 1936, Hiroshi Hara received his B.A. from the University of Tokyo (1959), his M.A. in 1961, and his Ph.D. from the same institution in 1964, before becoming an Associate Professor at the University's Faculty of Architecture. Though his first work dates from the early 1960s, he began his collaboration with Atelier f in 1970. Notable structures include numerous private houses such as his own residence, Hara House, Machida, Tokyo (1973–74). He participated in the 1982 International Competition for the Parc de la Villette, Paris; built the Yamato International Building (Ota-ku, Tokyo) in 1985–86; the Iida City Museum, Iida, Nagano (1986–88); and the Sotetsu Culture Center, Yokohama, Kanagawa (1988–90). Recent work includes the Umeda Sky Building (Kita-ku, Osaka 1988–93); and the Kyoto JR Railway Station (Sakyo-ku, Kyoto, 1990–97).

01/02 ITO HOUSE, Chijiwa, Nagasaki, Japan, 1997–98.
03 JR KYOTO RAILWAY, Station Kyoto, Japan, 1991–97.

01

02

ITSUKO HASEGAWA

"This is an interactive, tranquil, and meditative space, designed for the enjoyment of both the citizens of Niigata and visitors from around the world."

Itsuko Hasegawa was born in Shizuoka Prefecture in 1941. She graduated from Kanto Gakuin University in Yokohama in 1964. After working in the atelier of Kiyonori Kikutake (1964–69), she was a research student in the Department of Architecture of the Tokyo Institute of Technology. She was subsequently an assistant of Kazuo Shinohara in the same school (1971–78) before creating Itsuko Hasegawa Atelier (1979) in Tokyo. Her built work includes houses in Nerima (1986); Kumamoto (1986); and

01/02 NIIGATA PERFORMING ARTS CENTER, Niigata City, Niigata, Japan, 1993–98.

01

Higashitamagawa (1987). In more recent years, she has built on a larger scale: Shonandai Cultural Center (Fujisawa, Kanagawa, 1987–90); Oshima-machi Picture Book Museum (Imizu, Toyama, 1992–94) and the Sumida Culture Factory (Sumida, Tokyo, 1991–94). In 1995, she completed the University Gymnasium at Hikone, and the Museum of Fruit in Yamanashi. Itsuko Hasegawa was the runner-up in the 1993 competition for the new Cardiff Bay Opera House.

ZVI HECKER

"Architectural form cannot be derived from function alone, but must unfold within the confines of an artist's consciousness."

Born in 1931 in Krakow, Poland. Grew up in Krakow and Samarkand before moving to Israel in 1950. Studied architecture at Krakow Polytechnic (1949–50); Technion, Israel Institute of Technology, Haifa (1950–54), degree in engineering and architecture, 1955. Studied painting at Avni Academy of Art, Tel Aviv (1955–57). Two years military service in the Engineering Corps, Israeli Army. Set up private practice in 1959, working with Alfred Neumann until 1966 and Eldar Sharon until 1964. Buildings include: City Hall, Bat-Yam, Israel (1960–63); Club Mediterranée, Ahziv, Israel (1961–62); Aeronautic Laboratory, Technion Campus, Haifa, Israel (1963–66); Ramot Housing, Jerusalem, Israel (Phase 1 1974–76; Phase 2 1981–85); Spiral Apartment Building, Ramat Gan, Israel (1986–90). Recent projects include the Heinz-Galinski School, Berlin, the Palmach Museum of History, Tel Aviv, Israel and the Berlin Mountains residential neighborhood, East Berlin, Germany.

01/02 PALMACH MUSEUM OF HISTORY, Tel Aviv, Israel, 1992–98.

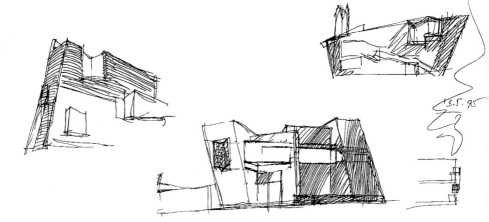

HERZOG & DE MEURON

The Swiss architects opted for an approach that conserves the rough, industrial qualities of Tate Modern, while providing 10,000 square meters of state-of-the-art exhibition space.

Jacques Herzog and Pierre de Meuron were both born in Basel in 1950. They received degrees in architecture at the ETH in Zurich in 1975 after studying with Aldo Rossi, and founded their firm Herzog & de Meuron Architecture Studio in Basel in 1978. Their built work includes the Antipodes I Student Housing at the Université de Bourgogne, Dijon (1991–1992); the Ricola Europe Factory and Storage Building in Mulhouse (1993); and a gallery for a private collection of contemporary art in Munich (1991–92). Most notably they were chosen early in 1995 to design the new Tate Gallery extension for contemporary art situated in the Bankside Power Station on the Thames, opposite Saint Paul's Cathedral (opened June 2000). They were also shortlisted in the competition for the new design of the Museum of Modern Art in New York (1997).

01

02

03

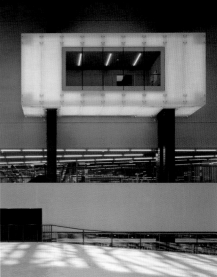

01/02 HOUSE, Leymen, France, 1996–97.
03/04 TATE MODERN, London, England, 1998–2000.

04

STEVEN HOLL

Born in 1947 in Bremerton, Washington. Trained at the University of Washington, 1970, in Rome, and at the Architectural Association in London (1976). Began his career in California and opened his own office in New York in 1976. Has taught at the University of Washington, Syracuse University, and, since 1981 at Columbia University. Notable buildings: Hybrid Building, Seaside, Florida (1984–88); Berlin AGB Library, Berlin, Germany, competition entry (1988); Void Space/Hinged Space, Housing, Nexus World, Fukuoka, Japan (1989–91); Stretto House, Dallas, Texas (1989–92); Makuhari Housing, Chiba, Japan (1992–97); Chapel of St. Ignatius, Seattle University, Seattle, Washington (1994–97); Kiasma Museum of Contemporary Art, Helsinki, Finland (1993–1998). Recent work includes the extension to the Cranbrook Institute of Science, Bloomfield Hills, Michigan (1996–99). Winner of the 1998 Alvar Aalto Medal, Steven Holl recently completed the Bellevue Art Museum, Bellevue, Washington, and is completing an expansion and renovation of the Nelson Atkins Museum of Art (Kansas City, Missouri). Other current work includes the Knut Hamsun Museum (Hamaroy, Norway); an Art and Art History Building for the University of Iowa (Iowa City, Iowa); and the College of Architecture at Cornell University (Ithaca, New York, 2004).

01 Y-HOUSE, Catskills, NY, USA, 1997–99. **02 KIASMA MUSEUM OF CONTEMPORARY ART**, Helsinki, Finland, 1993–98.

DAVID HOVEY

"The design integrates existing materials and systems from every industry rather than developing customized components to perform the same function."

Born in Wellington, New Zealand in 1944, David Hovey attended the Illinois Institute of Technology (1967–70) and worked as an Assistant Architect in the 20th Century Art Department at The Art Institute of Chicago (1967–70), before going to the offices of AS. Takeuchi (1971–74), and C.F. Murphy (1974–78). He created his present firm, Optima, Inc. in 1978. His work includes a number of multi-family residential

developments in Evanston, Wilmette, Deerfield, and Chicago, Illinois; mixed-use developments in Glenview, Wilmette or Highland Park, as well as single family prototype residences. David Hovey has been an Associate Professor of Architectural Design at the Illinois Institute of Technology since 1978.

ARATA ISOZAKI

"Every element is treated in a schizophrenic manner, so the whole becomes coherent."

Born in Oita City on the island of Kyushu in 1931, Arata Isozaki graduated from the Architectural Faculty of the University of Tokyo in 1954 and established Arata Isozaki & Associates in 1963, having worked in the office Kenzo Tange. Winner of the 1986 Royal Institute of British Architects Gold Medal, he has been a juror of major competitions such as that held in 1988 for the new Kansai International Airport. Notable buildings include: The Museum of Modern Art, Gunma (1971–74); the Tsukuba Center Building, Tsukuba (1978–83); The Museum of Contemporary Art, Los Angeles (1981–86); Art Tower Mito, Mito (1986–90); Team Disney Building, Florida (1990–94); Center for Japanese Art and Technology, Krakow, Poland (1991–94). B-con Plaza, Oita (1991–95). Current projects include Higashi Shizuoka Plaza Cultural Complex, Shizuoka; Ohio's Center of Science and Industry (COSI), Columbus, Ohio.

01/02 **SHIZUOKA, CONVENTION AND ARTS CENTER "GRANSHIP"**, Shizuoka, Japan, 1993–98. **03/04 COSI**, Columbus, Ohio, USA, 1994–99.

01

02

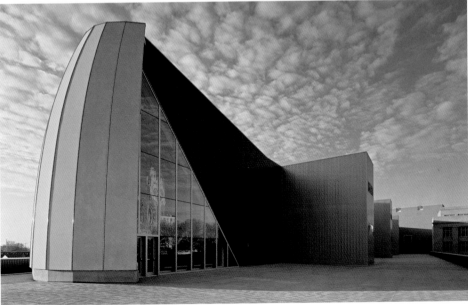

03/04

TOYO ITO

> "I always find myself back at Le Corbusier. I never consciously go back to him. It is only
> when I am already there ... that I realize what I have done."

Born in 1941 in Seoul, Korea, Toyo Ito graduated from the University of Tokyo in 1965, and
worked in the office of Kiyonori Kikutake until 1969. He created his own office in 1971, assuming the
name of Toyo Ito Architect & Associates in 1979. His completed work includes the Silver Hut residence
(Tokyo, 1984); Tower of the Winds (Yokohama, Kanagawa, 1986); Yatsushiro Municipal Museum (Yatsushiro, Kumamoto, 1989–91); and the Elderly People's Home (1992–94) and Fire Station (1992–95) both
located in the same city on the island of Kyushu. He participated in the Shanghai Luijiazui Center Area
International Planning and Urban Design Consultation in 1992, and has built a Public Kindergarten
(Eckenheim, Frankfurt, Germany, 1988–91). Recent projects include his Odate Jukai Dome Park (Odate,
Japan, 1995–97); Nagaoka Lyric Hall (Nagaoka, Niigata, Japan, 1995–97); and Ota-ku Resort Complex
(Tobu-cho, Chiisagata-gun, Nagano, 1996–98).

01 LYRIC HALL, Nagaoka, Niigata, Japan, 1993–96.
02/03 JUKAI DOME PARK, Odate, Japan, 1995–97.

JAKOB + MACFARLANE

The aluminum floor rises up to form four "sky grottoes" that house the kitchen, toilets, bar and VIP guest room.

Dominique Jakob received her degree in art history at the Université de Paris 1 (1990) before obtaining her degree in architecture at the École d'Architecture Paris-Villemin (1991). She has taught at the École Spéciale d'Architecture (1998–99) and the École d'Architecture Paris-Villemin (1994–2000). Born in New Zealand, Brendan MacFarlane received his Bachelor of Architecture at SCI-Arc (1984), and his Master of Architecture degree at Harvard, Graduate School of Design (1990). He has taught at the Berlage Institute, Amsterdam (1996), the Bartlett School of Architecture in London (1996–98), and the École Spéciale d'Architecture in Paris (1998–99). Both Jakob and MacFarlane have worked in the office of Morphosis in Santa Monica. Their main projects include the T House, La-Garenne-Colombes, France (1994,1998); the Georges Restaurant (Georges Pompidou Center, Paris, France, 1999–2000); and the restructuring of the Maxime Gorki Theater, Petit-Quevilly, France (1999–2000).

01/02 CENTRE GEORGES POMPIDOU RESTAURANT, Paris, France, 1998–2000.

VINCENT JAMES

The "type" referred to by the architect relates to the repeated use of rectangular volumes.
Each volume is then differentiated, explaining the term "variant."

Vincent James received his Master of Architecture degree from the University of Wisconsin in
Milwaukee in 1978. He worked as an intern at Hardy Holzman Pfeiffer Associates, 1978–80, and at
Chrysalis Corporation, 1980–84, before founding Vincent James Associates in 1994. He received a
National AIA Honor Award for the Type/Variant House in 1998. He has worked on the K.N. Dayton
Residence, Minneapolis, 1996–97; Brooklyn Children's Museum Master Plan, Brooklyn, New York,
1997–98; the Minneapolis Rowing Club, Minneapolis, Minnesota, 1998; and on the CALA Addition and
Remodeling, University of Minnesota, Minneapolis, with Steven Holl Architects, 1998.

01-04 TYPE/VARIANT HOUSE, Northern Wisconsin,
United States, 1994–97.

01

REI KAWAKUBO

"Without change nothing new can be born. Even a simple adjustment of the viewpoint can sometimes change everything dramatically."

Rei Kawakubo created the Comme des Garçons label in 1969 and established Comme des Garçons Co. Ltd in Tokyo in 1973. She opened her Paris boutique in 1982, and one in New York two years later. Although she is of course best known as a fashion designer, she has long had an interest in furniture and architecture. Rei Kawakubo introduced the Comme des Garçons furniture line in 1983. The flagship store in Aoyama, Tokyo, which she recently redesigned with the help of Takao Kawasaki (interior designer), Future Systems (architect/facade), Christian Asutuguevieille (art director/interior), and Sophie Smallhorn (artist/interior) was first opened in 1989. Rei Kawakubo received an Honorary Doctorate from the Royal College of Art, London, in 1997. The New York boutique was designed by Rei Kawakubo with Takao Kawasaki as well as Future Systems.

01 **COMME DES GARÇONS FLAGSHIP STORE**, Tokyo, Japan, 1999. 02 **COMME DES GARÇONS STORE**, New York, NY, USA, 1999.

KHRAS

"The design of the building borrows its inspiration from the typical solitary farmhouses of the area."

Jan Søndergaard was born in 1947. He attended the School of Architecture, Royal Academy of Fine Arts, Copenhagen (1979), the Copenhagen Advanced College of Building Technology (1972), and is a Master carpenter. He has been a partner of KHRAS architects since 1988. Nominated for the Mies van der Rohe European Award in both 1992 and 1994, he has designed the Danish Pavilion, Expo 92, Seville, Spain, the headquarters of Pihl & Son, Lyngby, Denmark, an extension of the Royal Danish Embassy in Moscow and headquarters for Bayer Denmark and Unicon Beton.

01/02 BANG&OLUFSEN HEADQUARTERS, Struer, West Jutland, Denmark, 1996–99.

01

WARO KISHI

Though the influence of Mies van der Rohe, this house is as much related to Japanese tradition as it is to European Modernism.

Born in Yokohama in 1950, Waro Kishi graduated from the Department of Electronics of Kyoto University in 1973, and from the Department of Architecture of the same institution two years later. He completed his post-graduate studies in Kyoto in 1978, and worked in the office of Masayuki Kurokawa in Tokyo from 1978 to 1981. He created Waro Kishi + K. Associates/Architects in Kyoto in 1993. He completed the Autolab automobile showroom in Kyoto in 1989; Kyoto-Kagaku Research Institute, Kizu-cho,

01-03 HOUSE, Higashi-Osaka, Osaka, Japan, 1995–97.

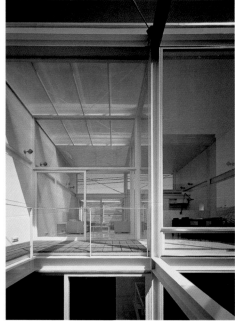

01

02

Kyoto in 1990; Yunokabashi Bridge, Ashikita-cho, Kumamoto, 1991; Sonobe SD Office, Sonobe-cho, Funai-gun, Kyoto, 1993; as well as numerous private houses. Recent work includes his Memorial Hall, Ube, Yamaguchi, 1997; a house in Higashi-nada, Kobe, 1997, and a house in Suzaku (Nara, Japan, 1997–98).

JOSEF PAUL KLEIHUES

Describing himself as a "poetic rationalist" in contrast with the Italian definition of the term, Kleihues seeks what he calls a "dialectic with Alberti, Palladio, Schinkel, and all the saints."

Born in 1933 in Rheine, Westphalia, Josef Paul Kleihues studied architecture at the Technische Universität Stuttgart and the Technische Universität Berlin from which he obtained a diploma (1955–59). He had a scholarship at the École des Beaux Arts, Paris, 1959–60, and worked afterwards with Hans Scharoun. He founded his own office in Berlin in 1962. As Professor at the University of Dortmund (Chair for Architectural Design and Theory, 1973–94) he created the Dortmund Architecture Days. He was the Planning Director for the 1984 Bauausstellung, Berlin (1979–84), and subsequently Consultant to the Senate for Housing and Construction in Berlin. His main works include the Berlin Cleansing Department, Main Workshop, Berlin-Tempelhof (1970–78); Block 270, Berlin (1975–77); Residential and Shopping Center, Neue Stadt Wulfen (1975–81); Hospital, Berlin-Neukölln (1975–86); Building 7, Block 7, Berlin (1988–89); Kant Triangle, Berlin-Charlottenburg (1992–94); Hamburger Bahnhof, Berlin (1992–96); Museum of Contemporary Art, Chicago, Illinois (1992–96). He created the firm Kleihues + Kleihues with his son Jan in 1996 and has worked more recently on projects in the Pariser Platz in Berlin. He was named Director of the Bauakademie in Berlin in 2001.

01/02 MUSEUM OF CONTEMPORARY ART, Chicago, Illinois, USA, 1992–1996. **03 HAMBURGER BAHNHOF,** Berlin, Germany, 1992–1996.

KOHN PEDERSEN FOX

Located at the Samsung Center, along the main road leading from the South Gate to Seoul City Hall, this 500 square meter glass pavilion was designed by Kevin Kennon of KPF.

KPF was founded in 1976. With offices in New York, London and Tokyo, KPF currently has work in thirty countries. The 206 person firm is led by the twelve principals: A. Eugene Kohn, FAIA, RIBA, JIA; William Pedersen, FAIA, FAAR; Robert L. Cioppa, FAIA; William Louie, FAIA; Lee Polisano, AIA, RIBA; David Leventhal, AIA; Gregory Clement, AIA; Paul Katz, AIA; James von Klemperer, AIA; Kevin Kennon, AIA; Michael Greene, AIA; and Peter Schubert, AIA. KPF's projects of note include the DG Bank Headquarters, Frankfurt (1993); the World Bank, Washington, D.C., (1996); IBM Corporate Headquarters, Armonk, New

01/02 RODIN PAVILION, Seoul, South Korea, 1995–97.

01

York (1997); and the Shanghai World Financial Center, Shanghai, (2004). Kevin Kennon, the Design Principal of the Rodin Pavilion, was born in 1958 and was educated at Princeton University and Amherst College. The attention to issues of transparency seen in the Rodin project is also featured in his other projects, such as the Sotheby's Headquarters in New York, the Morgan Stanley Headquarters at Rockefeller Center, New York, and the new prototype store for Bloomingdale's in San Francisco.

REM KOOLHAAS

"What if we simply declare there is not a crisis, redefine our relationship with the city not as its makers but as its mere subjects, as its supporters?"

Rem Koolhaas was born in The Hague in 1944. Before studying at the Architectural Association in London, he tried his hand as a journalist for the Haagse Post and as a screenwriter. He founded the Office for Metropolitan Architecture in London in 1975, and became well known after the 1978 publication of his book *Delirious New York*. His built work includes a group of apartments at Nexus World, Fukuoka (1991), and the Villa dall'Ava, Saint-Cloud (1985–1991). He was named head architect of the Euralille project in Lille in 1988, and has worked on a design for the new Jussieu University Library in Paris. His 1400 page book *S,M,L,XL* (Monacelli Press, 1995) has more than fulfilled his promise as an influential writer. Recent work includes a house, Bordeaux, France, 1998, movie studios in California and the campus center at the Illinois Institute of Technology, as well as the Guggenheim Las Vegas and the recent Prada boutique in the Soho area of New York.

01-03 EDUCATORIUM, UNIVERSITY OF UTRECHT, Utrecht,
The Netherlands, 1995–97.

KENGO KUMA

The intention of this project was to return the Noh Theater to its original environment – an outdoor setting.

Born in 1954 in Kanagawa, Japan, Kengo Kuma graduated in 1979 from the University of Tokyo with a Masters in Architecture. In 1985–86, he received an Asian Cultural Council Fellowship Grant and was a Visiting Scholar at Columbia University. In 1987 he established the Spatial Design Studio, and in 1991 he created Kengo Kuma & Associates. His work includes: the Gunma Toyota Car Show Room, Maebashi, 1989; Maiton Resort Complex, Phuket, Thailand; Rustic, Office Building, Tokyo; Doric, Office Building, Tokyo; M2, Headquarters for Mazda New Design Team, Tokyo, all in 1991; Kinjo Golf Club, Club House, Okayama, 1992: Kiro-san Observatory, Ehime, 1994; Atami Guest House, Guest House for Bandai Corp, Atami, 1992–95; Karuizawa Resort Hotel, Karuizawa, 1993; Tomioka Lakewood Golf Club House, Tomioka, 1993–96; Toyoma Noh Theater, Theater, Miyagi, 1995–96; and the Japanese Pavilion for the Venice Biennale, Venice, Italy, 1995. He has recently completed the Stone Museum (Nasu, Tochigi) and a Museum of Ando Hiroshige (Batou, Nasu-gun, Tochigi).

01

01-03 NOH STAGE IN THE FOREST, Toyama CITY, Toyama, Japan, 1996.

LAMOTT ARCHITEKTEN

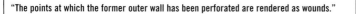

"The points at which the former outer wall has been perforated are rendered as wounds."

Ansgar Lamott was born in 1958 in Landau/Palatinate. He studied architecture at the University of Stuttgart (1978–85) and began to practice as an architect in 1985. A member of the architecture group Ostend 106 until 1996, he has taught at the University of Stuttgart (1994–96) and at the University College Biberach. He established his office with Caterina Lamott in 1996. Caterina Lamott (née Karakitsou) was born in 1956 in Athens, Greece. She studied at the University of Stuttgart, obtaining her diploma as an architect in 1981. She was also a member of the Ostend 106 group until 1996. The firm's projects, include an Elementary School in Hardthausen-Gochsen (1997); a Public Library in Landau (1996–98); a Sports Hall in Herxheim (1999); a Catholic Church Center in Völklingen/Saarland (2000); and a Music School in Fellbach (2000), all in Germany.

01-03 PUBLIC LIBRARY, Landau, Germany, 1996–98.

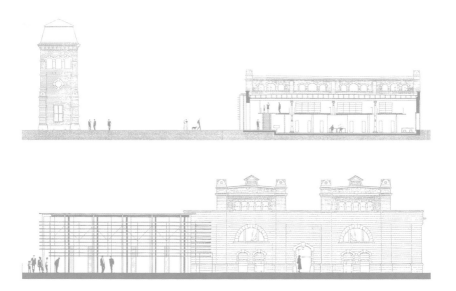

MAYA LIN

"Like a diamond in the rough, when you cut into it it reveals a more polished inner self."

Maya Lin attended Yale College and the Yale School of Architecture, receiving her Masters in Architecture in 1986. She created her office, Maya Lin Studio, in New York the same year. By that time, she had already created what remains her most famous work, the Vietnam Veterans' Memorial on the Mall in Washington D.C. (1981). Other sculptural work includes her Civil Rights Memorial in Montgomery, Alabama (1989), and "Groundswell," at the Wexner Center of the Arts, Columbus, Ohio (1993). Before the Langston Hughes Library and the Norton Residence, she completed the design for the Museum of African Art in New York (also with David Hotson, 1993); the Weber Residence, Williamstown, Massachusetts, 1994, and the Asia/Pacific/American Studies Department, New York University, New York, 1997. New work includes a Chapel for the Children's Defense Fund in Clinton, Tennessee.

01/02 LANGSTON HUGHES LIBRARY, Knoxville, Tennessee, USA, 1997–99.

DANIEL LIBESKIND

"It is the responsibility of architecture and culture to address events and history."

Born in Poland in 1946 and now a U.S. citizen, Daniel Libeskind studied music in Israel and in New York before taking up architecture at the Cooper Union in New York. He has taught at Harvard, Yale, Hannover, Graz, Hamburg, and UCLA. His work includes the Jewish Museum in Berlin, which is an extension to the Berlin Museum, 1992–99; and numerous proposals such as his 1997 plan to build an extension to the Victoria & Albert Museum in London, and his prize-winning scheme for the Bremen Philharmonic Hall, 1995. Like Zaha Hadid, Libeskind has had a considerable influence through his theory and his proposals, rather than his limited built work. The Felix Nussbaum Museum in Osnabrück, Germany, is in fact one of his first built, completed works. His current work includes a project for the Imperial War Museum, London, and for the Shoah Center in Manchester, England; the Jewish Museum, San Francisco, California; and the JVG University-Colleges of Public Administration, Guadalajara, Mexico.

01

01 FELIX NUSSBAUM MUSEUM, Osnabrück, Germany, 1996–98.
02/03 JEWISH MUSEUM, Berlin, Germany, 1989–99.

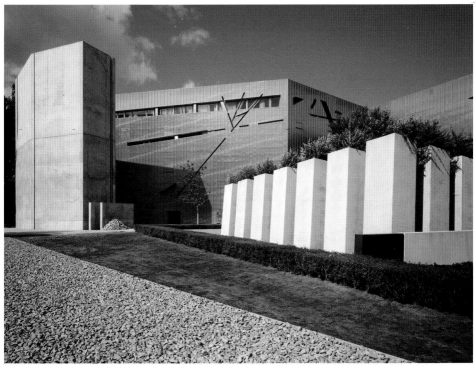

FUMIHIKO MAKI

Hillside Terrace is a testimony not only to Maki's talent as an architect, but to his ability to bring a civilized understanding of urban life into the midst of Tokyo's sprawling complexity.

Born in Tokyo in 1928, Fumihiko Maki received his B.Arch. degree from the University of Tokyo in 1952, and M.Arch. degrees from the Cranbrook Academy of Art (1953) and the Harvard Graduate School of Design (1954). He worked for Skidmore Owings and Merrill in New York (1954–55) and Sert Jackson and Associates in Cambridge, Massachusetts (1955–58), before creating his own firm, Maki and Associates in Tokyo in 1965. Notable buildings: Fujisawa Municipal Gymnasium, Fujisawa, Kanagawa (1984); Spiral, Minato-ku, Tokyo (1985); National Museum of Modern Art, Sakyo-ku, Kyoto (1986); Tepia, Minato-ku, Tokyo (1989); Nippon Convention Center Makuhari Messe, Chiba, Chiba (1989); Tokyo Metropolitan Gymnasium, Shibuya, Tokyo (1990); Center for the Arts Yerba Buena Gardens, San Francisco, California (1993). Recent projects include Nippon Convention Center Makuhari Messe Phase II, Chiba, Chiba, completed in 1997, and the Hillside West buildings completed in 1998, part of his ongoing Hillside Terrace project.

01 HILLSIDE WEST, Tokyo, Japan, 1996–98. **02 MAKUHARI MESSE**, Phase II, Nakase, Chiba, Japan, 1996–97.

MECANOO

"The new library takes the form of a building of glass and grass. It has a grass roof that rises at an angle from ground level, like a sheet of paper lifted at one corner."

Erick van Egeraat, Henk Döll, Chris de Weijer and Francine Houben in Delft created Mecanoo Architects in 1983. Döll and de Weijer were born in 1956, and Francine Houben a year earlier. All three attended the Technical University of Delft, graduating in 1983 and 1984. Their work included large housing projects such as the Herdenkingsplein in Maastricht (1990–92), and smaller scale projects such as their 1990 Boompjes Pavilion, a cantilevered structure overlooking the harbor of Rotterdam, close to the new Erasmus Bridge, or a private house in Rotterdam (1989–91). Signature features of these projects include unexpected use of materials, as in the Rotterdam house where bamboo and steel are placed in juxtaposition with concrete, for example, or an apparent disequilibrium, as in the Boompjes Pavilion. Erick van Egeraat left Mecanoo in 1995 with 17 members of the staff. Current projects of Mecanoo include a new 9,300 square meter library, music school and museum, Canadaplein, Alkmaar, 1997–2000; and an office for a housing association, Site Woondiensten, Doetinchem, 1998–2000.

01-03 CENTRAL LIBRARY, Delft Technical University, Delft, the Netherlands, 1993–98.

01

RICHARD MEIER

"I think that we live in a world culture. Countries' cultural identities no longer have the same meaning as they did in the past."

Born in Newark, New Jersey, in 1934. Richard Meier received his architectural training at Cornell University, and worked in the office of Marcel Breuer (1960–63) before establishing his own practice in 1963. He won the 1984 Pritzker Prize, and the 1988 Royal Gold Medal. His notable buildings include The Atheneum, (New Harmony, Indiana 1975–1979); Museum of Decorative Arts (Frankfurt, Germany, 1979–1984); High Museum of Art (Atlanta, Georgia, 1980–83); Canal Plus Headquarters (Paris, France, 1988–91); City Hall and Library (The Hague, Netherlands, 1990–1995); Barcelona Museum of Contemporary Art (Barcelona, Spain, 1988–1995); and the Getty Center (Los Angeles, California, 1984–97). Recent work includes the U.S. Courthouse and Federal Building (Phoenix, Arizona, 1995–2000).

01

02

01-03 NEUGEBAUER HOUSE, Naples, Florida, USA, 1995–98.

RAFAEL MONEO

The Auditorium and Congress Center are like "two gigantic rocks stranded at the river mouth that are part of the landscape, not the city."

Rafael Moneo was born in Tudela, Navarra, in 1937. He graduated from the Escuela Técnica Superior de Arquitectura in Madrid in 1961. The following year, he went to work with Jorn Utzon in Denmark. Rafael Moneo has taught extensively, including at the ETSA in Madrid and Barcelona. He was chairman of the Department of Architecture at the Graduate School of Design at Harvard from 1985 to 1990. His recent work includes the National Museum of Roman Art, Merida (1980–86), the San Pablo Airport Terminal in Seville (1989–91) built for Expo '92, the Atocha Railway Station in Madrid (1991), the Miró Foundation in Palma (1992); the interior architecture of the Thyssen-Bornemisza Collection in Madrid (1992); the Davis Museum at Wellesley College, Wellesley, Massachusetts (1993); Potsdamer Platz Hotel and Office Building, Berlin (1993–98); and concert halls in Barcelona (1999) and San Sebastián.

01-03 KURSAAL AUDITORIUM AND CULTURAL CENTER, San Sebastián, Guipuzcoa, Spain, 1990–99.

01

TOSHIKO MORI

The *Woven Inhabitation* may be "not only as a means to create contemporary shelter, but as a standard application for everyday building."

Toshiko Mori attended the Cooper Union School of Art and School of Architecture (1970–76), and received an Hon.M.Arch. degree from the Harvard School of Design in 1996. She is currently a Professor at Harvard. She has worked on numerous retail stores such as Comme des Garçons, New York, 1998; Kyoto Arts & Fashions, New York, 1989; as well as corporate offices such as Sony Research Laboratories, New York, 1996; or Nigel French International, New York, 1991. She completed the Issey Miyake Pleats Please Boutique with Gwenael Nicolas in the Soho area of New York in 1998.

01/02 WOVEN INHABITATION, New York, NY, USA, 1999.

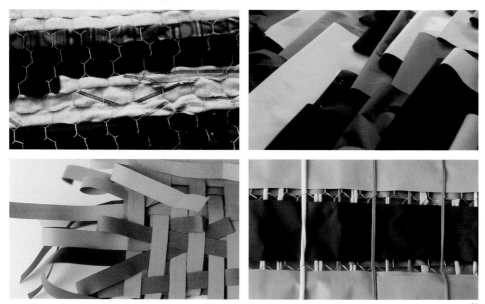

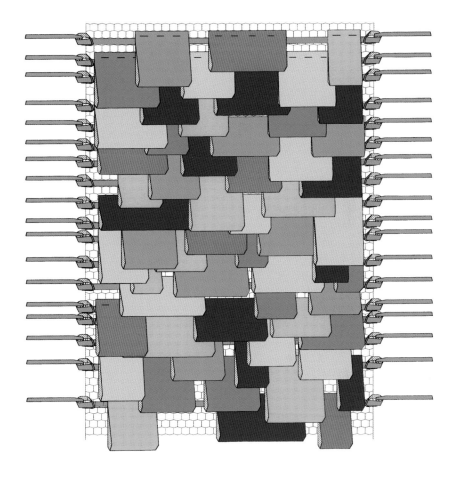

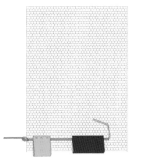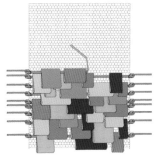

MORPHOSIS

"The business of architecture serves clients. You go out there and you find out what clients are interested in today. Real architecture is the antithesis of that."

Morphosis principal Thom Mayne, born in Connecticut in 1944, received his Bachelor of Architecture in 1968 at USC, and his Masters of Architecture degree at Harvard in 1978. He created Morphosis in 1979 with Michael Rotondi, who has since left to create his own firm, Roto. He has taught at UCLA, Harvard, Yale and SCI-Arc, of which he was a founding Board Member. Based in Santa Monica, California, some of the main buildings of Morphosis are the Lawrence House (1981); Kate Mantilini Restaurant (Beverly Hills, California, 1986); Cedar's Sinai Comprehensive Cancer Care Center (Beverly Hills, California, 1987); Crawford Residence (Montecito, California, 1987–92); Yuzen Vintage Car Museum (West Hollywood, California project, 1992), as well as the Blades Residence (Santa Barbara, California, 1992–97) and the International Elementary School (Long Beach, California, 1997–99). Current work includes the future Children's Museum of Los Angeles, which will be a key factor in the rejuvenation of Downtown Los Angeles, and serve as a landmark for the city. In addition, Morphosis is working on several significant public sector projects including a Federal Courthouse in Eugene, Oregon, the G.S.A. Headquarters building in San Francisco, and the NOAA Satellite Control Center in Washington D.C.

01-05 INTERNATIONAL ELEMENTARY SCHOOL, Long Beach, California, USA, 1995–98.

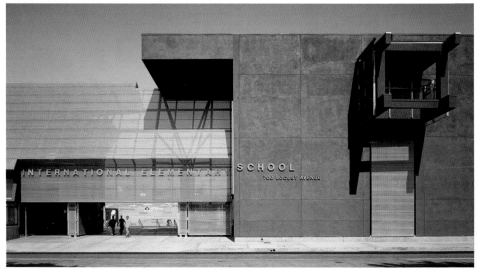

ERIC OWEN MOSS

"If the architecture could include oppositions, so that the building itself as an aspiration was about movement or the movement of ideas, then it might be more durable."

Born in Los Angeles, California, in 1943, Eric Owen Moss received his Bachelor of Arts degree from UCLA in 1965, and his Master of Architecture from UC Berkeley in 1968. He also received a Master of Architecture degree at Harvard in 1972. He has been a Professor of Design at the Southern California Institute of Architecture since 1974. He opened his own firm in Culver City in 1976. His built work includes the Central Housing Office, University of California at Irvine, Irvine (1986–89); Lindblade Tower, Culver City, (1987–89); Paramount Laundry, Culver City, (1987–89); Gary Group, Culver City, (1988–90), The Box, Culver City (1990–94); I.R.S. Building, Culver City (1993–94); and Samitaur, Culver City (1994–96). Current work includes high-rise towers in Los Angeles and a residential project in Hollywood, as well as ongoing designs in Culver City.

01-04 THE UMBRELLA, Culver City, California, USA, 1998–99.

GLENN MURCUTT

With concrete floors and walls, the center has a roof made of recycled timbers and steel under a corrugated galvanized iron roof sheet.

Glenn Murcutt was born in London in 1936 of Australian parents. He studied at the Sydney Technical College, University of New South Wales, and worked in the offices of Levido & Baker (1956) Neville Gruzman (1958–59) and Allen & Jack (1962) before creating his own office in 1969. He has taught at the University of New South Wales, and traveled extensively in Europe and the United States. His built work includes numerous private houses, such as the Magney House, Bingi Point, NSW, 1982–84; the Meagher House, Bowral, NSW; the Marika-Alderton House, Yirrkala Community, Eastern Arnhem Land, NT, 1991–94, as well as the Museum of Local History and Tourism Office, Kempsey, NSW, 1979–82, 1986–88; or a Restaurant, Berowra Waters, Sydney, 1977–78, 1982–83.

MVRDV

The raised grass covered roof tops what the architects call a "geological formation made up of the different floors," connected to each other by ramps in what amounts to a continuous space.

Winy Maas, Jacob van Rijs and Nathalie de Vries created MvRdV in 1991. The name of the firm is made up of the initials of the surnames of the partners. Born in 1959, Maas, like his two partners, studied at the Technical University in Delft. Jacob van Rijs was born in Amsterdam in 1964, and Nathalie de Vries in Appingedam in 1964. Both Maas and Van Rijs worked for OMA. Maas and de Vries worked in the office of Ben van Berkel before founding MvRdV. Aside from the Villa VPRO, their work includes the RVU Building in Hilversum, 1994–97; the Double House in Utrecht, 1995–97; as well as WoZoCos, 100 apartments for elderly people, Amsterdam-Osdorp, 1997. They have also worked on urban development schemes such as their "Shadow City Bergen Op Zoom" project, 1993, or the Masterplan for Parklane Airport, Eindhoven. The Villa VPRO bears some similarity to a 1993 project for a church in Barendrecht that evolved from a scheme involving "folded" shapes.

01/02 METACITY/DATATOWN, 1998–.
03/04 VILLA VPRO, Hilversum, the Netherlands, 1993–97.   03/04 ►

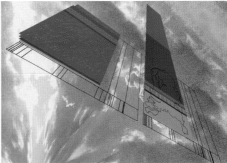

01

02

TAKEHIKO NAGAKURA

"This detective work coupled with virtual-practice experience is an extremely effective way of training and educating an architect."

Takehiko Nagakura is an architect from Tokyo. He received undergraduate education in architectural design under Professor Fumihiko Maki at the University of Tokyo and was a Ishizaka Memorial Foundation Scholar from 1985 to 1987 while he studied in the Master of Architecture program at Harvard University's Graduate School of Design. Currently, he is an Assistant Professor of Design and Computation at the Department of Architecture at the Massachusetts Institute of Technology. After

01 MONUMENT TO THE THIRD INTERNATIONAL, Petrograd, Soviet Union, 1919/1998.
02 PALACE OF THE SOVIETS, Moscow, Soviet Union, 1931/98.

01

graduation from GSD, Nagakura had a design practice in Japan, where he is a registered architect and engaged in building projects in Tokyo and Okinawa. His recent project for the Gushikawa Orchid Center was selected for SD Review Award in 1998, and is currently under construction in Okinawa. He heads the project UNBUILT, with research scientist Kent Larson, in which his team is developing computer graphics visualization of significant early modern unbuilt projects.

NEUTELINGS RIEDIJK

Willem Jan Neutelings was born in 1959 in Bergen op Zoop. He studied at the Technical University in Delft (1977–86) before working for the Office for Metropolitan Architecture with Rem Koolhaas (1977–86). He has taught at the Academy of Architecture in Rotterdam and at the Berlage Institute in Amsterdam (1990–99). Michiel Riedijk was born in Geldrop in 1964. He attended the Technical University in Delft (1983–89) before working with J.D. Bekkering in Amsterdam. He has taught at the Technical University in Delft and Eindhoven and at the Academies of Architecture in Amsterdam, Rotterdam and Maastricht. Their built work includes the Prinsenhoek Residential Complex, Sittard (1992–95); Tilburg Housing (1993–96); Hollainhof Social Housing, Gent, Belgium (1993–98); Borneo Sporenburg Housing, Amsterdam (1994–97); Lakeshore Housing, First Phase, Hulzen (1994–96); or the Building for Veenman Printers, Ede (1995–97).

01

01-03 MINNAERT BUILDING, Utrecht, Netherlands, 1994–97.

JEAN NOUVEL

Working with the noted landscape architect Gilles Clément and the lighting expert Yann Kersalé, Nouvel proposed a 7,500 square meter garden on the 2.5-hectare lot.

Born in 1945 in Sarlat, France, Jean Nouvel was admitted to the École des Beaux-Arts in Bordeaux in 1964. In 1970, he created his first office with François Seigneur. His first widely noticed project was the Institut du Monde Arabe in Paris (1981–87, with Architecture Studio). Other works include his Nemausus housing, Nîmes, (1985–87); offices for the CLM/BBDO advertising firm, Issy-les Moulineaux (1988–92); Lyon Opera House, Lyon (1986–93); Vinci Conference Center, Tours (1989–93); Euralille Shopping Center, Lille (1991–94); Fondation Cartier, Paris (1991–95); Galeries Lafayette, Berlin (1992–96); and his unbuilt projects for the 400 meter tall "Tour sans fin," La Défense, Paris (1989); Grand Stade for the 1998 World Cup, Paris (1994); and Tenaga Nasional Tower, Kuala Lumpur (1995). His largest recently completed project is the Music and Conference Center in Lucerne, Switzerland (1998–2000). He won both the competition for the Museum of Arts and Civilizations, Paris, and the competition for the refurbishment of the Reina Sofia Center, Madrid, in 1999. Current work includes plans for the Standard Hotel in Soho (New York) and a building for the Dentsu advertising agency in Tokyo.

01

02

01/02 CULTURE AND CONGRESS CENTER, Lucerne, Switzerland, 1992–99.
03 MUSÉE DU QUAI BRANLY, Paris, France, 2001–04.

03

NOX

> "The building is conceived as a dynamic system within which there is a constant, computer-mediated interaction between users, environment and building."

NOX is a cooperative venture between Lars Spuybroek, who was born in 1959 in Rotterdam, and Maurice Nio. Both studied at the Technical University in Delft. Their work has won several prizes (Archiprix 1990, Mart Stam Incentive Prize 1992) and has been supported by various grants (Enterprise Start-up Grants 1989 and 1992, Travel Grants 1992 and 1994, Work Grant 1994). Their work includes the Foam Home, a housing project for the KAN area near Nijmegen, 1997; OffTheRoad/103.8 Mhz, housing and noise barrier, Eindhoven, 1998; and the V_2 Engine, proposed facade for the V_2 Organization, Rotterdam,

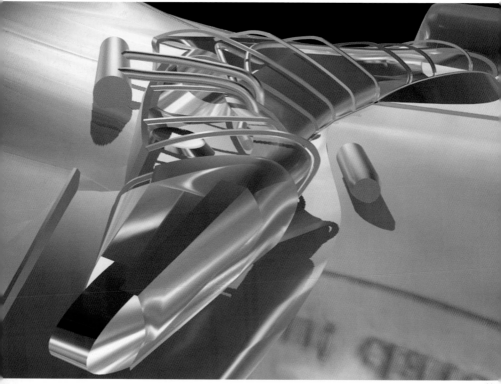

1997–98. Simultaneously with the formation of NOX-Architects, they created NOX-Magazine. Other activities include the translation of books into Dutch (Baudrillard, *Fatal Strategies*, and *America*), video productions (Belaagde Landen, Walvisspiegel, NOX' Soft City, Day-Glo LA), and installations (Armed Response, Den Bosch; Heavenly Bodies, Eindhoven). Lars Spuybroek and Maurice Nio regularly give talks and work as lecturers (Rietveld Academy, Amsterdam, Technical University Delft, and the architectural academies at Tilburg, Arnhem and Amsterdam). Lars Spuybroek is also editor of the journal *Forum*.

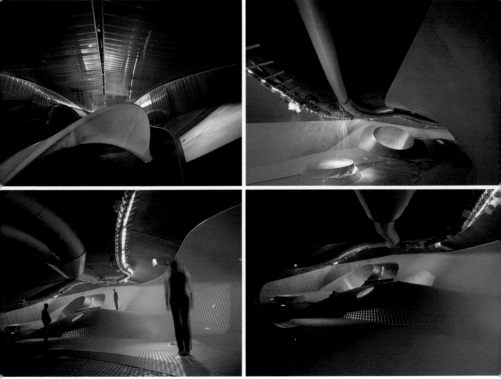

IEOH MING PEI

"Geometry came to my work early on because in the United States, the inner city is ordered by geometry. Geometry is a discipline, and I have been very disciplined."

Born in 1917 in Canton (now Guangzhou), China, I.M. Pei came to the United States in 1935. He received his Bachelor of Architecture degree from M.I.T. (1940); his Masters in Architecture from Harvard (1942); as well as a Doctorate at Harvard (1946). He formed I.M. Pei & Associates in 1955. He won the AIA Gold Medal (1979); the Pritzker Prize (1983); the Praemium Imperiale, in Japan in 1989. His notable buildings include: the National Center for Atmospheric Research, Boulder, Colorado (1961–67); the Federal Aviation Agency Air Traffic Control Towers, 50 buildings, various locations (1962–70); the John F. Kennedy Library, Boston, Massachusetts (1965–79); the National Gallery of Art, East Building, Washington, D.C. (1968–78); the Bank of China Tower, Hong Kong (1982–89); the Grand Louvre, Paris, France (1983–93); the Rock and Roll Hall of Fame, Cleveland, Ohio (1993–95), and the Miho Museum, Shigaraki, Shiga, Japan (1992–97). He collaborated with his sons (Pei Partnership) on the recent Bank of China Headquarters (Beijing, 1999– 2001). His current projects include a museum of modern art in Luxembourg, and a museum for Islamic Art in Doha, Qatar.

01-03 MIHO MUSEUM, Shigaraki, Shiga, Japan 1992–1997.

01

DOMINIQUE PERRAULT

Obviously intending to avoid the symbolism that accompanied the 1936 Games, Perrault opts for a minimalist discretion, a digging into the earth that is atypical of modernist designs.

Dominique Perrault was born in 1953 in Clermont-Ferrand, France. He received his diploma as an architect from the Beaux-Arts UP 6 in Paris in 1978. He received a further degree in urbanism at the École nationale des Ponts et Chaussées, Paris, in 1979. He created his own firm in 1981 in Paris. Recent and current work includes the Engineering School (ESIEE) (Marne-la-Vallée, 1984–87); the Hôtel industriel Jean-Baptiste Berlier (Paris, 1986–90); Hôtel du département de la Meuse (Bar-le-Duc, France, 1988–94); Bibliothèque Nationale de France (Paris, France, 1989–97); Olympic Velodrome, Swimming and Diving Pool (Berlin, Germany, 1992–98); and a large-scale study of the urbanism of Bordeaux (1992–2000). He is of course best known for his French National Library in Paris.

01-03 OLYMPIC SWIMMING POOL,
Berlin, Germany, 1992–99.

RENZO PIANO

"We often underestimate the immaterial aspects of space… sound, a certain vibration, light… I believe that light is space."

Born in 1937 in Genoa, Italy. Studied at University of Florence and at Polytechnic Institute, Milan (1964). Formed own practice (Studio Piano) in 1965, then associated with Richard Rogers (Piano & Rogers, 1971–1978). Completed Pompidou Center in Paris in 1977. From 1978 to 1980, Piano worked with Peter Rice (Piano & Rice Associates). Received RIBA Gold Medal, 1989. Created Renzo Piano Building Workshop in 1981 in Genoa and Paris. Built work includes: Menil Collection Museum (Houston, Texas, 1981–86), San Nicola stadium (Bari, Italy, 1987–90), 1989 extension for the IRCAM, Paris, and renovation of Lingotto complex, Turin; Mercedes-Benz Center (Stuttgart, 1992–96); Kansai International Airport Terminal (Osaka, Japan, 1988–94). Recent work includes: Cité Internationale de Lyon (Lyon, France, 1985–96); Jean-Marie Tjibaou Cultural Center (New Caledonia, 1994–98), and projects near the Potsdamer Platz in Berlin, as well as the New Metropolis Science Center, Amsterdam and Beyeler Foundation, Basel.

01/02 DEBIS TOWER, Berlin, Germany, 1993–99.
03 JEAN-MARIE TJIBAOU CULTURAL CENTER, Nouméa, New Caledonia, 1992–98.

01

02

POLSHEK PARTNERSHIP

The architect proposed to blow up the existing Hayden Planetarium and start over again.

James Stewart Polshek was born in Akron, Ohio, in 1930. He attended Case Western Reserve University (Cleveland, Ohio), graduating in 1951. He received his M. Arch. Degree from Yale in 1955 and established his own practice in New York in 1963. Recent projects include the renovation of Carnegie Hall (New York), the Center for the Arts Theater at Yerba Buena Gardens (San Francisco, 1993); a Government Office Building (Chambery-le-Haut, France); the Skirball Institute for Biomolecular Medicine and Residence Tower at New York University Medical Center (1993); the Seamen's Church Institute in the South Street Seaport Historic District (New York, 1991); and the renovation and expansion of the Brooklyn Museum of Art (New York). More recent work includes the Rose Center for Earth and Space, American Museum of Natural History (1997–2000) with his co-Design Principal on this project, Todd H. Schliemann; the Cooper Hewitt National Design Museum renovation and the Manhattan Supreme Court Criminal Courts Building, all in New York; and the National Museum of the the American Indian Cultural Resources Center in Suitland, Maryland. James Stewart Polshek was Dean of the Graduate School of Architecture, Columbia University, New York (1972–1987) until Bernard Tschumi succeeded him.

01/02 ROSE CENTER FOR EARTH AND SPACE, Frederick Phineas and Sandra Priest Rose Center for Earth and Space, American Museum of Natural History, New York, NY, USA, 1997–2000.

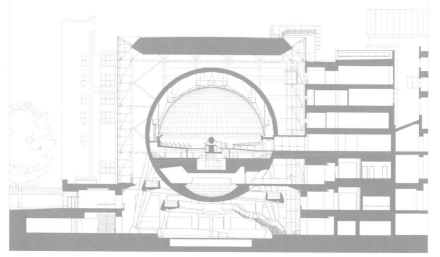

CHRISTIAN DE PORTZAMPARC

According to *The New York Times* Portzamparc reinvented the idea of Art Deco with this tower.

Christian de Portzamparc was born in Casablanca, Morocco, in 1944. He studied at the École des Beaux Arts, Paris (1962–69). Built projects include his Water Tower (Marne-la-Vallée, 1971–74); Hautes Formes public housing, (Paris, 1975–79); Cité de la Musique (Paris, 1985–95); Crédit Lyonnais Tower (Euralille, Lille, 1992–95) built over the new Lille-Europe railway station in Lille; Housing, Nexus World (Fukuoka, Japan, 1989–92); Extension for the Bourdelle Museum (Paris, 1988–92); and a Housing complex, ZAC Bercy (Paris, 1991–94). He was awarded the 1994 Pritzker Prize. Recent work includes the LVMH Tower on 57th Street in New York (1996–99); an addition to the Palais des Congrès in Paris (1996–99); a tower for the Bandai toy company in Tokyo; a courthouse for Grasse in the south of France; and a new concert hall in Luxembourg, as well as the French Embassy in Berlin due to be completed in 2003.

01/02 LVMH TOWER, New York, NY, USA, 1995–99.

ELISABETH DE PORTZAMPARC

The architect designed not only the space, but also the furniture for this restaurant.

Born in Brazil, Elizabeth de Portzamparc has been active in the area of design and architecture in Paris since 1975, when she did a study of the urban development of the Elancourt-Maurepas area of Saint-Quentin en Yvelines. She was Director of the Urban Planning Atelier of the city of Antony from 1977 to 1980. From 1988 to 1992, she created and directed the design gallery Mostra in Paris. She worked on the interior design of the Grasse Law Courts (1996–99) and is presently working on the interiors of the future French Embassy in Berlin (with Christian de Portzamparc). She was selected to design the station stops for the new Bordeaux tramway line, and is also working on the interior design and furniture for The Munt, a multiple screen movie theater in Amsterdam, and on the interiors of the Musée de la Bretagne in Rennes. She completed the Espionne boutique at the Palais des Congrès in Paris in 1999, and the Café de la Musique, also in Paris (1995), as well as numerous apartments.

01/02 LES GRANDES MARCHES RESTAURANT, Paris, France, 2000.   02 ►

RICHARD ROGERS

The largest roof in the world; big enough to engulf Trafalgar Square; one hundred times the size of Stonehenge, etc, etc.

Born in Florence, Italy, of British parents in 1933, Richard Rogers studied at the Architectural Association in London (1954–59). He received his Masters of Architecture degree from the Yale University School of Architecture in 1962. He created partnerships with his wife Su Rogers and Norman and Wendy Foster (Team 4, London, 1964–66); and with Renzo Piano in London, Paris and Genoa (1971–77). He created Richard Rogers Partnership in London (1977). He has taught at Yale, and been Chairman of the Trustees of the Tate Gallery, London (1981–89). Main buildings include: the Centre Georges Pompidou, Paris (with Renzo Piano, 1971–77); Lloyd's of London, Headquarters (1978–86); Channel 4 Television Headquarters, London (1990–94); Daimler Benz Office Building, Potsdamer Platz, Berlin (1993–99); Bordeaux Palais de Justice (1993–98).

01

01 LAW COURTS, Bordeaux, France, 1993–98.
02/03 MILLENNIUM DOME, London, England, 1996–99.

ROTO

"The architectural concepts were framed and shaped by the terms collaboration, dynamic systems and structures, and transformative processes."

Born in 1949 in Los Angeles, Michael Rotondi received his Bachelor of Architecture degree from the Southern California Institute of Architecture (Sci-Arc) in 1973. He worked with DMJM in Los Angeles (1973–76), and collaborated with Peter de Bretteville and Craig Hodgetts from 1974 to 1976. He was Director of the Graduate Design Faculty at Sci-Arc from 1976 to 1987. A principal of Morphosis with Thom Mayne (1980–92), Michael Rotondi has been the Director of Sci-Arc since 1987. He created his present firm, RoTo, with Clark Stevens in 1993. Stevens received his Masters in Architecture degree from Harvard in 1989, and worked at Morphosis beginning in 1987. Notable projects include CDLT 1,2, Cedar Lodge Terrace, Silverlake and the Teiger House (Somerset County, New Jersey, 1991–96); a Golf Club (Chiba Prefecture, Japan, 1988–92); the Sun Tower (Seoul, Korea, 1995–97). Recent projects include the Los Gatos Residence (Los Gatos, California); the Liberty Wildlife Center (Scottsdale, Arizona); and the Ontario Educational Village (Ontario California).

01-03 TEIGER HOUSE, Somerset Country, New Jersey, 1990–1995.

01

MIKE RUNDELL AND DAMIEN HIRST

"Art is about life and always has been. The art world is about money and always has been."

Mike Rundell & Associates was created in 1993 to produce architectural projects designed by Mike Rundell, who is best known as a sculptor and installation artist. Rundell was born in 1958 in London, and attended Oxford (1976–79) and the Camberwell School of Art (1986–89). He has completed twenty projects in the last three years, ranging from Tchaikovsky's flat in Saint Petersburg to a chain of hotels. Damien Hirst, born in 1965 in Bristol, is one of the best-known representatives of the so-called Young British Art. He lives and works in Devon. Winner of the 1995 Turner Prize with his controversial work "Mother and Child Divided," he has often placed an emphasis on what he calls the "healing power of art." His "spot paintings" with their "pharmaceutical" aspect make it clear that the theme of the restaurant he designed with Mike Rundell was no accident.

01-04 PHARMACY RESTAURANT, London, England, 1997–98.

03/04 ▶

01

02

SCHMIDT, HAMMER & LASSEN

The wavy design of the walls refers to the human, the body and the inner world of the soul.

Morten Schmidt, Joint Managing Director of SHL, was born in 1955 and graduated from the School of Architecture in Arhus (1982). He is in charge of the company's international projects. Bjarne Hammer was born in 1956 and is also a Joint Managing Director of the firm. In charge of projects for the Danish government, municipalities and service businesses, he graduated from the Arhus School of Architecture in 1982. John Lassen, born in 1953, also attended the Arhus School (1983) and is in charge of housing projects for SHL. The fourth Joint Managing Director is Kim Holst Jensen, born in 1964. Current work for the firm includes a new headquarters for Carlsberg; new headquarters for Andersen Consulting near Copenhagen Harbor; and 900 housing units for NCC Polska in Warsaw currently under construction.

01/02 EXTENSION OF THE ROYAL LIBRARY OF DENMARK, Copenhagen, Denmark, 1993–99.

01

AXEL SCHULTES AND CHARLOTTE FRANK

"A place of calm, which makes what is heavy clear and what is light possible."

Born in 1943 in Dresden, Axel Schultes graduated from the Technical University of Berlin in 1969. He worked in partnership with Dietrich Bangert, Bernd Jansen and Stefan Scholz from 1974 to 1991 (BJSS), with whom he built the Kunstmuseum Bonn. He created his own firm in 1992, and participated in both the Reichstag and Spreebogen competitions in 1993, as well as numerous other competitions before that such as that for the Alexandria Library in 1989, or the Potzdamer Platz in Berlin in 1991. The Spreebogen competition, which he won, was executed in collaboration with Charlotte Frank, born in Kiel in 1959, who has been his partner since 1992. His built work includes the Büropark am Welfenplatz, Hanover (1993). Recent projects are offices in Berlin, Leipziger Platz, and the Baumschulenweg Crematorium, Berlin.

01/02 BAUMSCHULENWEG CREMATORIUM, Berlin, Germany, 1992–98.

SCHWEGER + PARTNER

The ZKM Institute for Visual Media "sees itself as a forum for the creative and critical analysis of a constantly changing media culture."

Born in 1935 in Medias, Romania, Peter Schweger attended the Technical University, Budapest, and the University of Zurich, Edgenössiche Technische Hochschule Zurich (ETH), where he received his diploma in 1959. From 1959 to 1962 he had an office in Vienna. Research for the A. Körber-Stiftung, Hamburg (1960); visiting professorship at the Hochschule für Bildende Künste, Hamburg and at the Technical University of Hanover's Institute for Design and Architecture (1968–69). Founded office of Graaf

01/02 ZKM CENTER FOR ART AND MEDIA TECHNOLOGY, Karlsruhe, Germany, 1993–97.

01

+ Schweger in 1968 (1987 Architekten Schweger + Partner). Professor at the Technical University of Hanover, Institute for Design and Architecture (1972). Current work includes: Poseidon-Hause (office building), Hamburg (1990–95); Deutscher Industrie- und Handelstag (headquarters), Berlin (1994–97); and The Center for Art and Media Technology (ZKM), Karlsruhe (1993–97).

ALVARO SIZA

"Universality is not equivalent to neutrality, it is not the Esperanto of architectural expression, it is the capacity to create from the roots."

Born in Matosinhos, Portugal, in 1933, Alvaro Siza studied at the University of Porto School of Architecture (1949–55). He created his own practice in 1954, and worked with Fernando Tavora from 1955 to 1958. He has been a Professor of Construction at the University of Porto since 1976. He received the European Community's Mies van der Rohe Prize in 1988 and the Pritzker Prize in 1992. He built a large number of small-scale projects in Portugal, and more recently, he has worked on the restructuring of the Chiado, Lisbon, Portugal (1989–); the Meteorology Center, Barcelona, Spain (1989–92); the Vitra Furniture Factory, Weil-am-Rhein, Germany (1991–94); the Oporto School of Architecture, Oporto University (1986–95); and the University of Aveiro Library, Aveiro, Portugal (1988–95). His latest projects are the Portuguese Pavilion for the 1998 Lisbon World's Fair, and the Serralves Foundation, Porto, 1998.

01 SERRALVES FOUNDATION, Porto, Portugal, 1991–99.
02/03 PORTUGUESE PAVILION EXPO '98, Lisbon, Portugal, 1996–98.

01

SKIDMORE, OWINGS & MERRILL

Conceived before September 11, 2001, and intended to be the world's tallest building, 7 South Dearborn would have risen to a height of 473 meters and 108 stories.

Created in 1936, SOM has built in more than fifty countries. With offices in Chicago, New York, Miami, San Francisco, Los Angeles, London and Hong Kong, the firm is one of the largest of its type in the world. SOM has considerable experience in the area of tall buildings since completing the famous Lever House tower on Park Avenue in New York in 1954. The Sears and John Hancock towers in Chicago as well as the more recent Jin Mao Tower in Shanghai are all the work of SOM. The Design Partner for the 7 South Dearborn project is Adrian Smith, who joined SOM in 1969, and worked recently on the Jin Mao Tower as well as a number of other skyscrapers. William Baker is the Structural/Civil Engineering Partner, Raymond Clark the Mechanical and Electrical Engineering Partner, and Richard Tomlinson the Project Partner for 7 South Dearborn.

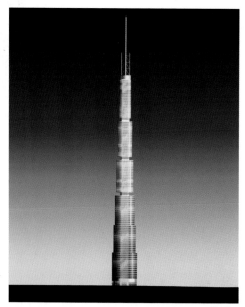

01/02 7 SOUTH DEARBORN, Chicago, Illinois, USA, 2000–03.

01/02 ►

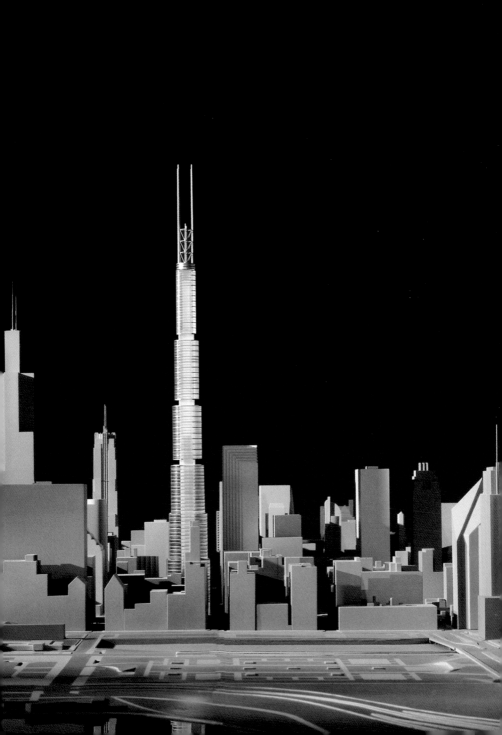

EDUARDO SOUTO MOURA

The architect was asked to create an exhibition gallery and an auditorium inside a spiral ramp that gives access to a parking area.

Eduardo Souto Moura was born in Porto, Portugal, in 1952. He graduated from the School of Architecture of Porto (ESBAP) in 1980. He was an Assistant Professor at the Faculty of Architecture in Porto (FAUP) from 1981 to 1991. He worked in the office of Alvaro Siza from 1974 to 1979 and created his own office the following year. Recent work includes Row Houses in the Rua Lugarinho, Porto, Portugal (1996); Renovation of the Municipal Market in Braga (1997); the Silo Norte Shopping Building; a house and wine cellar, Valladolid, Spain (1999); and the project for the Portuguese Pavilion, Expo Hannover (with Alvaro Siza, 1999). Current work includes the conversion of the building of the Carvoeira da Foz, Porto, and a project for the Braga Stadium.

01-03 SILO NORTE SHOPPING, Matosinhos, Portugal, 1998.

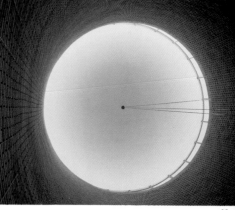

01

02

THOMAS SPIEGELHALTER

"I think the traditional division into art on this side and architecture on the other is quite obsolete and stifles communication between the various media."

Thomas Spiegelhalter was born in Freiburg in 1959. He works in Freiburg as a "sculptor, architect and communications designer." In 1977 he received a Venice Scholarship to study sculpture. He obtained degrees in Sculpture, 3-D Visual Communication and Architecture in Bremen, Flensburg and from the Hochschule der Künste in Berlin. He has taught architecture and visual arts in Kaiserslautern and at the Technischen Hoschscule in Leipzig. His projects include a number of sculptural works, sometimes related to his interest in the Freiburg gravel pits. Since 1989, he has worked on the design of energy efficient homes.

01/02 EXPERIMENTAL HOUSING, Freiburg, Germany, 1996–97.

PHILIPPE STARCK

"We have to replace beauty, which is a cultural concept, with goodness, which is a humanist concept."

Philippe Starck was born in 1949 and attended the École Nissim de Camondo in Paris. He is of course best known as a designer of objects such as chairs or lamps. He has always had an interest in architecture, however. His architectural and interior design projects include the Café Costes, Paris, 1984; Royalton Hotel, New York, 1988; Laguiole Knife Factory, Laguiole; Paramount Hotel, New York, 1990; Nani Nani Building, Tokyo, 1989; Asahi Beer Building, Tokyo, 1989; the Teatriz Restaurant, Madrid, 1990; and the Baron Vert building in Osaka, 1990. He has worked on a number of hotels with Ian Schrager, including the Saint Martin's Lane Hotel and the Sanderson Hotel, also in London.

01-03 TASCHEN PARIS BOOKSHOP, Paris, France, 2001.
2, Rue de Buci, F–75006 Paris

02/03 ►

01

SHIN TAKAMATSU

The museum has three pools designed to reflect the nearby Daisen Mountain. Takamatsu likens these reflections to the act of "pulling scenery into architecture."

Born in Shimane Prefecture in 1948, Shin Takamatsu graduated from Kyoto University in 1971 and from the Graduate School of the same institution in 1979. He created his own office in Kyoto in 1975. He has taught at Kyoto Technical University and at the Osaka University of Arts. Profiting amply from the building boom of the 1980s, Takamatsu completed a large number of structures including Origin I, II and

01/02 SHOJI UEDA MUSEUM OF PHOTOGRAPHY, Kishimoto, Tottori, Japan, 1993–95.

III (Kamigyo, Kyoto, 1980–86); the Kirin Plaza Osaka, (Chuo, Osaka, 1985–87); and Syntax (Sakyo-ku, Kyoto, 1988–90). In his more recent, less mechanical style, Takamatsu has completed the Kirin Headquarters (Chuo-ku, Tokyo, 1993–95); the Shoji Ueda Museum of Photography (Kishimoto-cho, Tottori, 1993–95); and the Nagasaki Port Terminal Building (Motofune-cho, Nagasaki, 1994–95).

YOSHIO TANIGUCHI

"The main buildings I have designed… are the result of combining simple but contradictory figures, namely centripetal and centrifugal forms, and space and mass."

Yoshio Taniguchi was born in Tokyo in 1937. He received a Bachelor's degree in Mechanical Engineering from Keio University in 1960 and a Master of Architecture degree from the Harvard Graduate School of Design in 1964. He worked in the office Kenzo Tange from 1964 to 1972. He created Taniguchi, Takamiya and Associates in 1975, and Taniguchi and Associates in 1979. His built work includes the Tokyo Sea Life Park, Tokyo, 1989; Marugame Genichiro-Inokuma Museum of Contemporary Art and Marugame City Library, Marugame, 1991; Toyota Municipal Museum of Art, Toyota City, 1995; the Tokyo Kasai Rinkai Park View Point Visitors Center, Tokyo, 1995; the Tokyo National Museum Gallery of Horyuji Treasures, Tokyo, 1997.

01-03 TOKYO NATIONAL MUSEUM, GALLERY OF HORYUJI TREASURES,
Tokyo, Japan, 1994–99.

TEN ARQUITECTOS

"TEN's insistent overlayering of the designed and the spontaneous... aims at the realization in architecture's elementary terms of a new, and nuanced paradoxality of living." *Lebbeus Woods*

Enrique Norten was born in Mexico City in 1954, and graduated as an architect from the Universidad Iberoamericana there in 1978. He received a Masters degree in Architecture from Cornell University in 1980. He was a partner in Albin y Norten Arquitectos (1981–85) before founding Ten Arquitectos in 1986. Bernardo Gomez-Pimienta was born in Brussels in 1961. He studied at the Universidad Anahuac in Mexico City and at Columbia. He has been a partner in Ten Arquitectos since 1987. Their built work includes a Cultural Center, Lindavista, 1987–1992; the National Theater School, Churubusco, 1993; and a workers Restaurant, San Angel, 1993. Recent work includes House Le, Mexico City, Mexico, 1995 and the Museum of Sciences, Mexico City, Mexico, 1997.

01-03 TELEVISA SERVICES BUILDING, Mexico City, Mexico, 1993–95.

01

02

BERNARD TSCHUMI

"The point is to be aware of theoretical issues and to start from a project, aiming at making connections with important ideas of our time."

Bernard Tschumi was born in Lausanne, Switzerland, in 1944. He studied in Paris and at the Federal Institute of Technology (ETH), Zurich. He taught at the Architectural Association, London (1970–79), and at Princeton (1976–80). He has been Dean of the Graduate School of Architecture, Planning and Preservation at Columbia University in New York since 1984. He opened his own office, Bernard Tschumi Architects (Paris, New York), in 1981. Major projects include: Parc de la Villette (Paris, France, 1982–95); Second prize in the Kansai International Airport Competition, 1988. Video Gallery (Groningen, The Netherlands, 1990); Le Fresnoy National Studio for Contemporary Arts (Tourcoing, France, 1991–97); Lerner Student Center, Columbia University (New York, 1994–98); School of Architecture (Marne-la-Vallée, France, 1994–98); and the Interface Flon railroad station in Lausanne, Switzerland.

01/02 LERNER HALL STUDENT CENTER, Columbia University, New York, NY, USA, 1994–99.
03/04 SCHOOL OF ARCHITECTURE, Marne-la-Vallée, France, 1994–99.

01

02

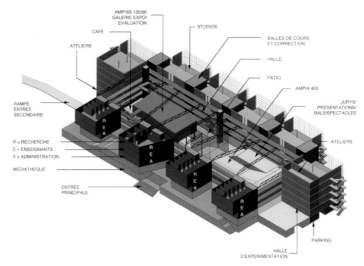

AMPHIS 135/90
GALERIE EXPO/
EVALUATION

CAFE

ATELIERS

STUDIOS

SALLES DE COURS
ET CORRECTION

HALLE

PATIO

AMPHI 400

RAMPE
ENTREE
SECONDAIRE

JURYS/
PRESENTATIONS/
BALS/SPECTACLES

R = RECHERCHE
E = ENSEIGNANTS
A = ADMINISTRATION

ATELIERS

MEDIATHEQUE

ENTREE
PRINCIPALE

PARKING

HALLE
D'EXPERIMENTATION

UN STUDIO

Here, in what Ben van Berkel calls a "bridge for an ordinary place," three decks open and close asynchronously "imitating the movement of playing fingers."

Ben van Berkel was born in Utrecht in 1957 and studied at the Rietveld Academie in Amsterdam and at the Architectural Association (AA) in London, receiving the AA Diploma with honors in 1987. After working briefly in the office of Santiago Calatrava, in 1988, he set up his practice in Amsterdam with Caroline Bos. In 1998, they created UN Studio, a subsidary which is a network of specialists in architecture, urban development an infrastructure. Van Berkel has been a Visiting Professor at Columbia, New York, and Visiting Critic at Harvard, 1994. He was a Diploma Unit Master at the AA, London, 1994–95. As well as the Erasmus Bridge in Rotterdam (inaugurated in 1996), Van Berkel & Bos Architectural Bureau has built the Karbouw and ACOM (1989–93) Office Buildings, and the REMU Electricity Station (1989–93), all in Amersfoort, housing projects, and the Aedes East gallery for Kristin Feireiss in Berlin. More recent projects are the Möbius House, Naarden (1993–98); Het Valkhof Museum, Nijmegen and an extension for the Rijksmuseum Twente, Enschede (1992–96); a Music Facility, Graz, Austria (1998–2002); and a Switching Station, Innsbruck, Austria (1998–2001). Ben van Berkel and Caroline Bos recently won the competition to expand and renovate the Wadsworth Atheneum Museum of Art.

01 MÖBIUS HOUSE, 't Gooi, The Netherlands, 1993–97.
02 BASCULE BRIDGE AND BRIDGEMASTER'S HOUSE, Purmerend, Netherlands, 1995–98.

01/02 ►

MAKOTO SEI WATANABE

The one-story steel frame structure juts out over a neighboring river. The architect also created a technological garden that he calls "Edge of Water."

Born in 1952 in Yokohama, Makoto Sei Watanabe attended Yokohama National University from which he graduated with a Master's Degree in Architecture in 1976. In 1979, he went to work for Arata Isozaki & Associates, and in 1984, he established Makoto Sei Watanabe/Architects' Office. His first work, the Aoyama Technical College built in the Shibuya-ku area of Tokyo in 1989, brought him international attention because of its spectacular forms influenced by cartoon graphics. His other work includes: Chronospace (Minato-ku, Tokyo, 1991); Mura-no-Terrace gallery, information office and cafe, Sakauchi Village (Ibi-gun, Gifu, 1995); Fiber Wave, environmental art (Gifu and Tokyo, 1995–96); Atlas, housing, (Suginami-ku, Tokyo, 1996); K-Museum (Koto-ku, Tokyo, 1996); Fiber Wave, environmental art, The Chicago Athenaeum (Chicago, 1998); and the Iidabashi Subway Station (Tokyo, 1999–2000).

01/02 MURA-NO TERRACE, Ibi-gun, Gifu, Japan, 1994–95.

01/02 ▶

WILLIAMS AND TSIEN

This house was intended to satisfy the client's request for a "quiet serenity, an openness to the landscape and a sense of spaciousness without monumentality."

Tod Williams, born in Detroit in 1943, Bachelor of Arts, 1965, Master of Fine Arts, 1967 Princeton University. After six years as associate architect in the office of Richard Meier in New York, he began his own practice in New York in 1974. He taught at the Cooper Union for more than 15 years and has also taught at Harvard, Yale, the University of Virginia, and Southern California Institute of Architecture. Tod Williams received a mid-career Prix de Rome in 1983. Billie Tsien was born in Ithaca, New York, in 1949. She received her Bachelor of Arts at Yale, and her Masters of Architecture from UCLA (1977). She has been a painter, and graphic designer (1971–75). She has taught at Parsons School of Design, Southern California Institute of Architecture (SCI-ARC), Harvard and Yale. Their built work includes: Feinberg Hall (Princeton, New Jersey, 1986); New College, University of Virginia (Charlottesville, Virginia, 1992), as well as the renovation and extension of the Museum of Fine Arts in Phoenix (Arizona, 1996). Recent projects include the Williams Natatorium – phase 1 for the Cranbrook Academy (Bloomfield Hills, Michigan); the Museum of American Folk Art in New York, and the Johns Hopkins University Student Art Center (Baltimore, Maryland).

01

02

01/02 NEW YORK CITY HOUSE, New York, New York, United States, 1995-97.
03/04 RIFKIND HOUSE, Georgica Pond, Long Island, New York, USA, 1997-98.

JEAN-MICHEL WILMOTTE

Located in the Pyung Chang Dong area of Seoul, this 2,000 square meter facility includes exhibition space, a cafeteria, bookshop, conference room, outdoor theater and a sculpture garden.

Born in 1948, a graduate of the Camondo school in Paris, Jean-Michel Wilmotte created his own firm, Governor, in 1975. Although he is best known for his work in interior design, including private apartments for François Mitterrand in the Élysée Palace, Wilmotte joined the Order of Architects in France in 1993. His recent work includes the architecture and interior design of the Decorative Arts Department of the Louvre, Richelieu Wing, (1989-1993), and the Museum of Fashion, Marseille. As an architect, Jean-Michel Wilmotte recently completed the International Executive Office building, Tokyo, and the New N°3 Arai building, also in Tokyo, while also carrying out the furniture design for the Banque de Luxembourg building, completed by Arquitectonica in 1994.

01-06 GANA ART CENTER, Seoul, South Korea, 1996-98.

01

02

03/04/05/06

KEN YEANG

The most striking feature of the building is its 2,500 square meter wing-shaped inflatable fabric canopy.

Born in 1948 in Penang, Malaysia, Ken Yeang attended the Architectural Association in London (1966–71) and Cambridge University (Wolfson College, 1971–75). Much of his subsequent work was based on his Ph.D. dissertation in Cambridge on ecological design. His work (with Tengku Robert Hamzah as TR Hamzah & Yeang created in 1976 in Kuala Lumpur) includes the MBF Tower (Penang, 1990–93); the Menara Mesiniaga Tower (1989–92), a recipient of the 1995 Aga Khan Award; a tower in Ho Chi Minh City (Vietnam, 1992–94); the Tokyo-Nara Tower (Japan, 1997); and the Menara UMNO (Penang, 1998). His published books include *The Architecture of Malaysia*, Pepin Press, Kuala Lumpur, 1992, and *The Skyscraper, Bioclimatically Considered: A Design Primer*, AD, London, 1997. Ken Yeang was President of the Malaysian Institute of Architects from 1983 to 1986.

01-04 GUTHRIE PAVILION, Shah Alam, Selangor, Malaysia, 1995-98.

01

02

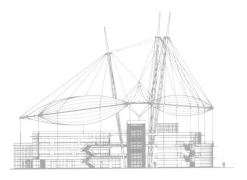

SHOEI YOH

This 30 by 32 by 32-meter observation tower was "conceived as a midair museum dedicated to the beauty of the earth and the universe."

Born in 1940 in Kumamoto City, Shoei Yoh received a Degree in Economics from Keio Gijuku University, Tokyo (1962), and studied Fine and Applied Arts at Wittenberg University in Springfield, Ohio (1964). Self-trained as an architect, he opened Shoei Yoh + Architects in Fukuoka in 1970, and gained a local reputation in industrial and interior design. His Stainless-Steel House with Light Lattice (Nagasaki, 1980) was widely published. More recent work such as his Kanada Children Training House (Tagawa, Fukuoka, 1994) and his Uchino Community Center for Seniors & Children (Kaho, Fukuoka, 1995) show his flair for spectacular forms, which draw, in their sense of space or in certain techniques, on Japanese tradition. Shoei Yoh is a Professor of Architecture and Urban Design at the Graduate School of Keio University.

01/02 PROSPECTA '92 TOYAMA OBSERVATORY TOWER, Kosugi, Toyama, Japan, 1990-92.

CREDITS

IMPRINT

© 2002 **TASCHEN GMBH**
Hohenzollernring 53, D–50672 Köln
www.taschen.com

EDITORIAL COORDINATION Sonja Altmeppen, Cologne
TEXT EDITOR Malcom Green, Heidelberg
LAYOUT Claudia Frey, Cologne
PRODUCTION Thomas Grell, Cologne
COVER DESIGN Claudia Frey and Angelika Taschen, Cologne

Printed in Italy
ISBN 3–8228–2507–7

COVER
Alberto Campo Baeza, Center for Innovative Technologies BIT, Inca, Majorca, Spain
© Hisao Suzuki

Building a New Millennium
Philip Jodidio
Flexi-cover, 560 pp.

Architecture Now! Vol. I
Philip Jodidio
Flexi-cover, 576 pp.

Architecture Now! Vol. II
Philip Jodidio
Flexi-cover, 576 pp.

"TASCHEN books are beautiful, original,
unpredictable, and affordable." —*The Observer Life Magazine*, London

" Buy them all and add some pleasure to your life."

All-American Ads 40^S
Ed. Jim Heimann

All-American Ads 50^S
Ed. Jim Heimann

Angels
Gilles Néret

Architecture Now!
Ed. Philip Jodidio

Art Now
Eds. Burkhard Riemschneider,
Uta Grosenick

Atget's Paris
Ed. Hans Christian Adam

Best of Bizarre
Ed. Eric Kroll

Bizarro Postcards
Ed. Jim Heimann

Karl Blossfeldt
Ed. Hans Christian Adam

California, Here I Come
Ed. Jim Heimann

50^S Cars
Ed. Jim Heimann

Chairs
Charlotte & Peter Fiell

Classic Rock Covers
Michael Ochs

Description of Egypt
Ed. Gilles Néret

Design of the 20th Century
Charlotte & Peter Fiell

Designing the 21st Century
Charlotte & Peter Fiell

Dessous
Lingerie as Erotic Weapon
Gilles Néret

Devils
Gilles Néret

Digital Beauties
Ed. Julius Wiedemann

Robert Doisneau
Ed. Jean-Claude Gautrand

Eccentric Style
Ed. Angelika Taschen

Encyclopaedia Anatomica
Museo La Specola, Florence

Erotica 17th–18th Century
From Rembrandt to Fragonard
Gilles Néret

Erotica 19th Century
From Courbet to Gauguin
Gilles Néret

Erotica 20th Century, Vol. I
From Rodin to Picasso
Gilles Néret

Erotica 20th Century, Vol. II
From Dali to Crumb
Gilles Néret

Future Perfect
Ed. Jim Heimann

The Garden at Eichstätt
Basilius Besler

HR Giger
HR Giger

Indian Style
Ed. Angelika Taschen

Kitchen Kitsch
Ed. Jim Heimann

Krazy Kids' Food
Eds. Steve Roden,
Dan Goodsell

London Style
Ed. Angelika Taschen

Male Nudes
David Leddick

Man Ray
Ed. Manfred Heiting

Mexicana
Ed. Jim Heimann

Native Americans
Edward S. Curtis

New York Style
Ed. Angelika Taschen

**Extra/Ordinary Objects,
Vol. I**
Ed. Colors Magazine

15th Century Paintings
Rose-Marie and Rainer Hagen

16th Century Paintings
Rose-Marie and Rainer Hagen

Paris-Hollywood
Serge Jacques
Ed. Gilles Néret

Penguin
Frans Lanting

Photo Icons, Vol. I
Hans-Michael Koetzle

Photo Icons, Vol. II
Hans-Michael Koetzle

20th Century Photography
Museum Ludwig Cologne

Pin-Ups
Ed. Burkhard Riemschneider

Giovanni Battista Piranesi
Luigi Ficacci

Provence Style
Ed. Angelika Taschen

Pussy-Cats
Gilles Néret

Redouté's Roses
Pierre-Joseph Redouté

Robots and Spaceships
Ed. Teruhisa Kitahara

Seaside Style
Ed. Angelika Taschen

Seba: Natural Curiosities
I. Müsch, R. Willmann, J. Rust

See the World
Ed. Jim Heimann

Eric Stanton
Reunion in Ropes & Other
Stories
Ed. Burkhard Riemschneider

Eric Stanton
She Dominates All & Other
Stories
Ed. Burkhard Riemschneider

Tattoos
Ed. Henk Schiffmacher

Edward Weston
Ed. Manfred Heiting